DON'T YOU KNOW

LOVE WINS IN THE END

By Pastor C.L. Fitzgerald

AuthorHouse™
1663 Liberty Drive
Bloomington, IN 47403
www.authorhouse.com
Phone: 833-262-8899

Because of the dynamic nature of the Internet, any web addresses or links contained in this book may have changed since publication and may no longer be valid. The views expressed in this work are solely those of the author and do not necessarily reflect the views of the publisher, and the publisher hereby disclaims any responsibility for them.

Any people depicted in stock imagery provided by Getty Images are models, and such images are being used for illustrative purposes only.
Certain stock imagery © Getty Images.

This book is printed on acid-free paper.

ISBN: 979-8-8230-2235-4 (sc)
ISBN: 979-8-8230-2237-8 (hc)
ISBN: 979-8-8230-2236-1 (e)

Library of Congress Control Number: 2024903469

Print information available on the last page.

Published by AuthorHouse 02/16/2024

authorHOUSE®

DON'T
YOU
KNOW

THE TRUTH ABOUT LOVE, LIFE, AND OUR CREATION
INTO THIS VERY EXISTENCE,

BY
Pastor C.L. Fitzgerald

I was born May 19th, 1972, yay go Taurus! I have had a lot of things happen to me in this life. This autobiography is very true and solid and offers plenty of evidence and valid facts. I was born May 19th, 1972, in the city of Danville VA. Danville VA sits in Pittsylvania County. Pittsylvania county is the largest land mass county in Virginia this is where I called home. Blair's Virginia and Kentuck Virginia and Keeling Virginia and Ringgold Virginia these are communities within the Pittsylvania County boundaries where I was raised up in.

I was told by my mother that t was born with no name. My mother had planned on me being born a girl that was what she thought I would be a girl, But God's will be that I was born a boy. My mother has a baby doll the same age as I am. She purchased the doll anticipating me being born a girl. My mother tells me that the nurse asked her when I was born, what his name was going to be and my mother replied she didn't know.

Fortunately for me there was a TV show on in her room. The show was called Julia starring Diane Carroll. In the TV show called Julia starring Diane Carroll, Diane Carroll plays a nurse with a son that stays into mischief and always into something.

Now in this show Julia Mrs. Carroll son's name is Corey Baker. That's what my mother named me. I can imagine from after being exhausted from having me, she pointed to the little boy on the TV and said name him Corey.

Personally, I love the name Corey, it's very distinctive and fits me very well. Don't you know God worked it out perfectly for me? I grew up as a young boy, very poor, my family and I as it seems. I was the second to the youngest of 10 children. My mother said that when she met my daddy that he had lost his wife and was left to raise 5 little children. My mother had three children when they met these are my older brothers and sisters. So, my daddy had three girls and two boys, and my mother had two boys and one girl when my mother and father met. Together my mom and dad had me, Corey lee Fitzgerald and my younger sister who was born September 18, 1974.

Joyce Lillian Fitzgerald is my youngest sister. Don't you know that I remember just like as if it's today, I remember when my sister came home from the hospital after she was born.

The day my sister came home it was a very rainy day with a thunderstorm with lots of heavy rain. I remember oh so well. I remember seeing my mother walk through the front door holding my sister in her car seat. I was so excited to see my sister and I remember that I no longer felt alone, I was all smiles and very happy that day. I remember my mother putting the car seat on the Bed yet with my sister still in it, and I remember my mother picking me up placing me on the bed right beside her and then I looked into my sister's beautiful brown eyes, and she was looking back at me.

I could see my mother seemed to be very exhausted at this point, see my mother had to go into the kitchen to wash up a sink full of dirty dishes. Yes, I remember very clearly when I asked my mother can i hold her, my mother looked at me and said OK you can hold her. It was chili outside and it was raining and thundering and lightning very hard and more consistently at this point. So, my mother said that I could hold my sister and I was overjoyed. My mother told me to sit back on the bed and she took my sister out of her car seat. My mother then said hold out your arms and she placed my sister into my arms. I remember just like it was yesterday my mother said very clearly and plain she said watch her while I go into this kitchen and wash up these dishes.

Don't you know I just sat there on the bed and just held my baby sister, and she looked up at me with the most amazingly beautiful brown eyes and she has her pacifier in her mouth. I just held her while looking at all that rain rolling down the windowpane looking out the window. Don't you know to my surprise, as if out of nowhere a huge bolt of lightning hit just outside the window unexpectedly. It scared me so bad. I remember very much remember when that flash of lightning hit, my sister went flying out of my arms up in the air and I jumped up in the bed and amazingly I watched her as something gently laid her down on the floor! I could not believe nor understand what I had just witnessed but, anyway my sister was just crying on the floor, and I heard my mother in the kitchen say in a very loud tone, " Lord what now".

My mother came out of the kitchen and picked up my sister up off the floor and placed her back in her car seat on the bed and told me to sit there and watch her while she washed up all the dishes. From that point on all my life up until today I am and always have been afraid of Thunder and lightning, but what was this that just safely placed my sister on the floor after I dropped her because if my sister had hit the floor after me tossing her up in the air, she would not have survived that in my opinion.

Well, there were many great memories as my sister, and I started to grow we had to grow up fast I remember some good days as well as not so good days. My brothers and sisters were much older than me and my sister Joyce I remember them teaching me how to ride a bike I would beg them to let me ride their 10 speed bike so they would take turns sitting me up on that bike and they would hold the seat and guide me around in a circle on their bike, and my sister Joyce and I would set out on the porch and watch my older brothers and my uncles play basketball all day long till my mother got home from work.

Never in my life as long as I live will I ever forget having to fetch a 5-gallon bucket of water for me and my family. I had not even started school yet and my mother and I, and Joyce, would go to the spring wetl to get a bucket of water to drink and to take bath with. I can see my mother with a 5-gallon bucket of water in each hand and my sister carried her baby doll while I would be struggling with this one five-gallon bucket of water. I was not big, so I let the bucket of water swing between my legs while I walk and strain to get this bucket of water home; I even came up with a little rhythm to help me along my walk. I would say right leg swing bucket, left leg swing bucket, that was my rhythm as we walked up the hill from the well on our way home. Don't you know all the years, all the seasons of going through that path down the hill to get to the well to fetch water for the family to drink and take a bath, my sister and my mother and I we never saw a snake but once and he was just going into the bushes as he crossed the path. It's funny; being little by the time we get home I would not have even 1/2 a bucket of water because my water would be splashing out as I walked and swing the bucket.

I'm from the country, I was born and raised that way. one thing I enjoyed when I was little, we had what we call a woodpile. One thing I happily loved to do is when the big truck would bring firewood, the wood came in the form of big, long planks so this truck would bring the firewood and I would just sit there to wonder and watch as the truck swiftly backed up to the wood pile and in reverse, come to an abrupt stop and the wood slid off the truck, Being a little boy that always fascinated me.

As time passed, I began to slowly grow. There were ten of us children growing up, I remember very well. We lived in some very old houses and these old houses were cold in the wintertime. It would be so cold sometimes we all have to get in the same bed to stay warm. I remember in the wintertime with the ice and snow on the ground you could look down through the floor and see the snow blowing under your feet.

My dad works for the city of Danville water treatment plant and my mother works cleaning houses for people. My dad only drove cars that he could work on. He loved working on cars and most of them he fixed didn't work. One day my mother had to go to the store to buy some food and my dad drove one of those cars that wouldn't work most of the time. so, my dad Drove my mother who sat in the passenger seat my sister who sat in the back seat and myself who was in the back seat as well We were in the car heading to the grocery store. On the way to the store, we had to cross some train tracks. It was a very beautiful day.

Everything was going well until we got to the train tracks and then as we attempted to cross the train track that old car cut off right on the tracks My dad attempted to restart that old car, but it would not start. over and over, he would turn the switch to try to get it to start but it would not start.

Suddenly, the cross guard started to come down with the lights flashing on the cross guards that warns you that a train is coming, and I could see the train in the distance coming around the bend. Closer and closer the train came. I looked at my mother and she was praying very hard, my dad kept trying to start that old car and my sister had a very disgraceful look upon her face. I Was jumping up and down in the back seat of that old car as the train got closer and closer it had become so close and I could see the driver as he covered his eyes as to prepare for an impact. While in the back seat of this car jumping up and down a large man figure appeared, and it looked at me and gave a big shove with both of his arms and that car jumped the track.

I had fallen on the floor of this car and when I got up and looked the train had just missed us. After the train passed by a white elderly gentleman who was traveling behind us got out of his car and ran up to our car and asked if everyone was OK, he was so excited this man walked up to my daddy's window and said did y'all see that, did y'all see that! The gentleman went on to explain that an Angel came out of the sky and hit that car and made it jump the train track he witnessed it all. My dad just looked at the man and laughed and the gentleman slowly turned around and walked back to his car with his head down, I continue to jump up and down in the back seat of the car. I was so happy because I witnessed it as well and I knew what had just happened at this very young age. To be honest there were some very hard times growing up in a large family. I remember my mother and dad not getting along too well and mental abuse can be just as bad as physical abuse to a kid and to an adult.

My mother and my dad not getting along and my mother working hard cleaning up people's houses and my dad working for the city, but we didn't see much of his money. I remember a lot of times on Friday my dad would get drunk, and he had a lot of women in his life this made my mother mad and bitter as it should. My sister Joyce and I had to cope with a lot in our young life.

I remember my sister and I used to love to play in the dirt and make pancakes and cakes out of the dirt and even needed sometime. We just made life the best we could, being that our older brothers and sisters moved out eventually on their own. The very first school we attended was called Mount Hermon school. This school was K through 12th grade. We attended the school with our older brothers and sisters, but we didn't attend it long before they would eventually close it down and separate the kids, due to older kids. At mount Hermon my sister Joyce and I felt like we were little ants, it seemed like the other kids were giants. One day a kid in the first grade kept picking on me for getting an F on my assignment; he kept saying Corey got an F, Corey got an F, he made a little song out of it and that really made me mad. While singing his little song I reached back and hit him in the face and broke his nose. My older sister was passing by the door and saw me hit this kid, and the kid turned out to be my cousin.

Growing up at this stage in my life we didn't have much to eat and I thank God for always feeding me and my brothers and sisters. One thing that I am very glad about living in these old houses that should have been abandoned, there was an apple tree and a pear tree and a Peach tree right there by where we waited to catch the bus every morning, we had our choice of fruit for breakfast. one day an elderly white gentleman was passing by the road while we were waiting on our bus, and he stop and ask if he could pick some of the fruit. While picking his fruit I remember him saying he had never seen a tree bear fruit in the wintertime. Don't you know these trees around our house bear fruit all year long we even have walnut trees and pecan trees as well. I remember very well as if it was today, having to practice a fire drill on the bus. They don't do it today, but we used to have to practice jumping out the back of the bus through the emergency door. It was a fun experience and scary experience at the same time. I thank God for all and every schoolteacher I ever had in my life and principle as well.

I think back to kindergarten there was a girl named Priscilla in my class that sat in the desk right in front of me. Priscilla was loved by all the teachers and all the students. Her smile alone brightened the classroom and she made everyone laugh and was a joy to be around. she had long brunette hair that came down the middle of her back so when every time she set in front of me her hair would be on my desk; I will never forget everyday playing with her hair I would take my pencils and roll and wrap her hair up using my pencils. Then I can hear my teacher saying everyday she say,

Corey Leave Priscilla 's hair alone and we laugh, but Priscilla told the teacher she said I don't mind Corey's not bothering me. We all got along like family. Well one day after going home from school I remember going home and I could hear my mother talking on the phone about a bad accident that had happened involving a dump truck. So, at this time it was like a tradition to watch the 6:00 news as most people does. I was intrigued to see the news this night with my mother just to see what had happened. well, the news came on and there was breaking news there was a deadly crash on the highway involving a dump truck and a car with a woman and three kids never will I ever forget watching and hearing this terrible news.

The dump truck was at fault for hitting the car and the new said the lady and her three kids we're killed in this car accident. My mother said Lord have mercy, and all I can think is that I pray that it was no one that I knew. Well the very next day got up and went to school and when I got to school all the kids came into the room but I did not see Priscilla. The desk in front of me was empty. The teacher took a chair and sat in the middle of the class and told us to come and sit Indian style in a circle. I remember looking at her face and seeing tears come down. The teacher said she had some very bad news to tell us, and I knew what was coming next. Yet I'm looking at the front door to the classroom to see in hopes of Priscilla coming in the classroom and the teacher began to tell us that Priscilla and her mother and her sister and brother had been involved in a car accident and that she would not be in class anymore.

My heart fell into the pit of my stomach I knew what had happened the kids started to ask questions like when would she be back the teacher said Priscilla had been killed in a car accident I remember all the kids crying and screaming and it was a very sad situation, the nurse and the principal saying to us if anybody needs counseling for us to go to the office ; the entire class and school was not the same after that. This class was a family we loved and cared about each and everyone.

Don't you know I have had some of the greatest teachers and influences in my life growing up like this one time the holidays was approaching it was Thanksgiving coming up and the HBO channel was giving a national contest for schools across the United States every week on HBO they would present a school each week on their special presentation program.

My kindergarten teacher entered my class in this HBO contest, and I could not believe our class won the contest. I was so happy when she told us I told my mother when I got home from school that I was going to be on TV. I remember we had to meet and the Danville Public Library early in the morning around about 2:00 AM to do the taping for the HBO special presentation the boys and the girls we were all dressed up like little Indians and little pilgrims our teacher had us singing a song for Thanksgiving and it was so beautiful they filmed us, and we were going to be featured on HBO. Now at this time my family we did not have cable we were still using a black and white TV set. My uncle on my dad's side of the family was the only one we knew that had cable so when the HBO special aired, we had to go over to their house to see it. Everybody was so excited and waiting with so much anticipation to see the show my uncles wife seemed the most excited because she loved me and my sister Joyce so much I can hear her saying to everyone in the room y'all be quiet its coming on so when the presentation aired on HBO there I was dressed up like a little Indian singing this song everybody was just smiling and laughing I was looking tired and sleepy And I can remember hearing her say look at Corey look at Corey that was a great time 'Ell always remember.

After my mother could not take any more of my dad drinking and women my mother took my older sister than me and Joyce and we get our own place. We moved to Keeling, Virginia. I will be going to Kentucky elementary school Joyce and me. There was this one special Christmas wear my daddy got me a BMX bike I really like that bike. Well at Kentucky elementary school I stayed in a lot of trouble more than a normal kid and I was the class clown. I don't know how I passed my grades. My mother had to meet with the teachers a lot about my grades and my conduct. I remember getting a lot of whippings. My mother was very frustrated somehow, I managed to graduate to my next school which would be called Dan River middle school as I am starting to grow in statue. I had to learn how to be the man of the house in this house in Keeling was very questionable it was an old house as well as we have become accustomed to This old house in Keeling VA sits up in the middle of a field where wheat would grow. This old house had no running water. It was a haunted house seems to me. My two sisters and I would walk up the road maybe 100 yards to the bus stop. Snakes have always been my biggest fear. I remember my mother one day getting all the clothes together to watch them as I was throwing the clothes down the steps so she could wash them in that old washing machine I seen the clothes moving on their own. stopped and told my mother that the clothes were moving, and she knew what it was a long, big black snake came out it was wrapped up in the clothes. My mother called her brother to come over and remove the snake from inside the house. He was in the Navy and snakes didn't scare him.

I am terrified of snakes. Like this one day f went to get a 5gallon bucket of water from the well right outside of the house, It had a well that you had to pump and prime the water faucet to get a bucket of water and I noticed the ground under me was moving. I looked down and it was a giant water moccasin snake, and I ran into the house. A lot happened at this old house, but I really enjoyed riding my BMX dirt bike up and down the driveway my sister and I would take turns riding it. We also had an old black and white TV set during this time, and I found my outlet in watching TV and listening to music.

I will never forget one night, it was very hot during the summer, and my family and I were watching TV. We had an old electric fan blowing the heat around it was setting up in the window.

Wefå, this night t was laying in the floor watching TV and the door was open but the screen door with closed and locked. I remember I looked up at the screen door and jumped up in frantic haste. Don't you know that was a taål black man standing at the screen door looking down at me. My mother goes to the door to see what the man wanted, and he asked for a glass of water. She gave him a cup of water and he walked away. My mother and I watched him walk away off the porch and before he got to the end of the porch don't you know this man vanished in air. My mother looked at me and said, "did you see that"?

Like I said before a lot of strange and unusual questionable things happened at this house which was located in Keeling Virginia. Meanwhile at school I was still acting up and in class not paying attention to my teachers. My very first time going to the circus was in Dan River middle school. The circus was called the Ringling brothers and Barnum and Bailey circus and was at the Greensboro Coliseum in North Carolina. was beyond excited this day. I had a chance to see the world's tallest man and the world's smallest man on the same stage. Outside the Coliseum they allowed us to pet the elephants and see all of the wild animals. Also at Dan river middle school I got to go to Asheboro zoo in North Carolina and amazing zoo and will always remember and never forget going to colonial Williamsburg VA to Jamestown that was exciting.

It bothered me to the core of my soul to see my mother work so hard to provide for me and my two sisters. My mother worked cleaning people's homes and worked in the tobacco field all day long from 4:00 to 5:00 AM in the morning till about 5-6 and seven in the evening she worked. There were other men and women and Mexicans pulling tobacco as well. After school she would pick up me and my sister Joyce up at the house when we got out of school and then we would go with her back to the tobacco fiefd and sit in the car till she got offp then when we were out of school for the summer. Joyce, and I was sitting in the car for 13 till 14 hours while my mother worked pulling tobacco.

My sister and I would listen to music all day long in the car. Country music and gospel music we knew every country song and gospel song on the radio this was our normal routine. I could not wait to get older and grow some more so that I could help my mother provide for us. will see my mother work herself so hard at the end of the day her hands would be so black with the tar from the tobacco leaves. My mother would have to wash her hands and gasoline to break down the tar, before she could wash them with soap.

I continue to be the class clown and ultimately held back a grade the teachers said they would hold me back to being the same grade as my sister. they said that Joyce could help me with my work and maybe by doing this I wilt make better grades and it will be a big help to me.

A man is very, very important in a young boy's fife, and never had that figure. had to learn and figure things out all on my own. Ali my life I was told that I had very beautiful handwriting, by my teachers. [ended up finding love and a passion and an outlet for drawing. And became very good until my drawings caught the attention of my teachers. My teacher at Dan River middle school came to me and said that there was going to be a drawing contest and she wanted me to enter it. The theme was going to be Christmas, so I done a poster picture of Santa Claus on the Danville trolley going downtown tossing out gifts to all the girls and boys.

Don 9t you know not only did my picture win first prize and had a blue ribbon attached to it, but my picture was posted in the local Danville register and bee newspaper also. My poster was placed in the window of a store downtown right at Christmas for all to see. I was so proud of myself. It seems that I was the only one proud of me and that can be troubling at times. As young children we look to our parents for approval and sometimes we never get it.

So now I thank God I became 15 years old at this point and can work part time to help my mother out. with afl my heart thank God for Mr. Parker, after he talked to my mother, he offered me a job pulling tobacco. Mr. Parker was a very good man and that's who we farmed with and who gave me my first job. "YES"! I no longer had to sit in the hot car and watch my mother work so hard but, now I can work and help out around the house, and I was so thankful. I no longer had to wear clothes that my mother brought home of somebody that had passed away that she cleaned the house for. We did not have to eat food any longer from people that didn't won't the old, stale food from when she cleaned the refrigerator at her job. It felt good to buy me and my sister Joyce school clothes and shoes. As far as school goes, a lot of things happen at Dan River middle school but now my sister Joyce and I are headed to junior high school So, my mother, my two sisters and \ move from keeling Virginia to a little better house on state route 729 in Ringgold VA. Blairs junior high school would be the next school that Joyce and I attended and would be the best school I ever attended. I thank God yet again for the teachers believing in me and seeing something in me. My sister Joyce was in the choir at the school and my older sister was in high school and had her sights on going to a four-year College and furthering her education.

Why you ask me, that Blairs middle school would be my best school? I Em glad you asked me, I learned how to drive at a driving range while at Blairs middle school. I was beginning to obtain some freedom and learning how to drive so when I got to high school that would really help me.

I was very fit and in shape at this point in my life and love the game of basketball. My favorite subject was PE. One day during the summer in our PE class our teacher took the class outside and set up a high jump for everybody to take turns jumping over this pole. All the boys and girls were taking turns jumping over the pole getting eliminated left and right because each run the bar started to go up higher and higher.

There it was, it had come down to just me and another guy left to jump. I beat this guy by jumping over 7 feet 11 inches tall. I know this may sound unbelievable to most, but the coach moves that bar up to 8 feet and four inches and asked me if I can jump over it and t replied yes, I can. remember very' clearly how I got a good running start and jumped over that bar, Coach looked at me and said you just broke the world record; I cant believe it myself. The coach explained to me that had broken the world record for the high jump, and he said that he would notify the world record people and then would need a trainer and that he would work with me as well. My heart became crushed and devastated because the first thought in my mind was that we could not afford a trainer and that broke my heart. It has become so very painful to think about the fact that I broke the world record for the high jump, and it wasn 't legally recorded. Blairs junior high school is where a lot of things in my life happened good and bad, but it was time to complete junior high school and move up into the big leagues and go on to high school.

But before high school I remember one day my sister Joyce and me and my mother. We all love corn on the cob. So, one day we each get a 5-galåon bucket and went to the field to pick us some corn for dinner, this lady that my mother cleaned house for let us pick corn out of her garden. We got out of the car when we got to the field and started picking corn and putting it into our buckets. My mother had noticed that every time we moved something would move also. Joyce and I were too busy playing and laughing at each other and really didn't notice the sound. White picking corn and playing and having a good time my mother said "yᵛa[l be quiet". I knew right then that something was not right, my mother stood up to look up, and then bent down very quickly. Dont you know I jumped up over the corn to see if I could see what my mother had seen and then I got down. What I saw was a black snake looking around for us. This snake was so huge and long it stood up on its tail and was taller than the corn. My heart fell into the pit of my stomach, I can hear my mother saying yᵗall run to the car!

I remember telling my mother to come on and we all took off running to that old red Ford Granada car. We ran as fast as we could, the three of us, and we jumped in that old car and as my mother drove off, I looked out the back window and could see that snake come out as if it was looking for us, and it had to be at least 15 feet long. Then my mother went back to the lady's house to tell her what had happened.

I remember the start of high school. Dan river high school home of the Wildcats Ringgold VA. My mother, Joyce, and I attended an open house to meet our teachers and to get our classes and curriculum, t stilå would have that same old attention disorder where I didn't want to pay attention in class but that was getting better. These four years of high school would most definitely prove to me who I am and would bee My high school years would be 1989;1990; 1991 and 1992. My favorite classes would be drivers' education, PE, and English literature. love poetry and poems.

Meanwhile f found a joy in going to church every Sunday my mother taught my sister and I how to give every Sunday in service and to mean it from the depth of our heart. She told us that whatever we do for God to let it be real. our home church at this time would be called" Greater Triumph Baptist Church in Chatham VA where the late Doctor H.G. McGee was our pastor, and he also baptized my sister and me.

I love an honor this church and my pastor as I was getting to know God my creatore After church one of my favorite things to do besides eating would be to watch a good old Elvis Presley movie that came on every Sunday around 2:00 PM. My pastor the late doctor HG McGee loved God and he loved people. He knew a tot of people. I remember the parents of the great tennis player, Arthur Ashe junior, coming to our church and speaking. That was so rememberable.

Not only did Arthur ash junior family come to our church, but I also remember the great pastor Jerry Falwell, founder of Liberty University in Lynchburg VA coming to our church and giving a sermon as well. A lot of great and memorable things took place at my home church.

One day I had got home from school and my sister, and I was in the front yard playing basketball because we had a Basketball court in our front yard. I was showing her how high I can jump and would dunk the ball and she would smile at me jumping. I was the best at dunking a ball, I thought. When we got tired, we went inside and got some water and watched TV and just relaxed. I remember my mother was cooking some good food and the house was smelling so good, cornbread and chicken and Pinto beans.

I went to my room to listen to some music and around about 6:00 PM I will never forget the phone rang and I answered it because I was waiting on my girlfriend from school to call me. Well, when I answered the phone, I said hello, but nobody said nothing, so I said hello again and this little boy said I'm going to kill myself. my heart fell into the pit of my stomach. I was 16 years old and did not know what to do. I asked the little voice on the other end of the phone why do you want to kill yourself? The little boy said 1 ¹m going to kill myself. I was not a counselor nor did I have a doctor's degree, but don't you know God use me Started to talk to this young man, I found out that he was 12 years old he told me his name and we talked about everything we talked about school and cars that he like. He told me that his dad left him and his brother and sister and mother. As time went on, I remembered my mother said don't have the phone she was expecting a phone call, and the phone did beep and let me know that a call was coming in, but I did not answer. I was too afraid to let this young man go up the phone well from 6:00 PM till about 10:00 PM we talked, and the call dropped. was so scared and fearful for this young man but thank God the phone rang, and it was my friend.

I asked him t said how do you remember the number and this young man said I just hit redial. Thank God he found a comfort in talking to me because I like talking to him as well. could see my sister and my mother getting ready for bed and my mother kept looking at me and then once asked me did any call come through and I had to reply and say no. So, we continued to talk all night long around 2:00 AM to 3:00 AM. I became very sleepy, but I just wanted him to keep talking to me. It was now Saturday morning, and the time was 7:00 AM.

My friend and I talked all night long. I heard the front door open and the lady's voice she called him his name and I could hear her walk over to him and she asked him what he was doing on the phone, and my friend said 1 ¹m talking to this guy. Well, his mother took the phone, and she said hello.

I was so glad! I told her, your son called this number and told me he was going to kill himself. She seen that he had her sleeping pills and a glass of water sitting on the table beside the phone. Again, my heart fell into the pit of my stomach because this was not a joke, he really was going to kill himself by taking her sleeping pills. I could hear the boy's mother just crying and just crying. She came back on the phone and said Sir thank you for talking to my son all night long. She went on to say Sir is there anything I can do for you, and I replied please get your son some help please.

She promised me that they would all get help and counseling. She told me that her husband left her, and she had been working three jobs to provide for them then she thanked me again and again and we hung up. God is amazing. With no training nor degree of any kind, and just 16 years old, God used me to save a young man's life. As time went on, I found two more outlets in my life to go along with music and a good movie. One would be poetry and the other literature. That's why I say I thank God for my teachers because they taught me a lot and math was not a strong subject for me at all but English and grammar was. My English teacher got us into William Shakespeare and Edgar Allan Poe and poems. became very good at understanding poetry and short stories. Understood what the writers were thinking and going through. One day our English teacher wanted us to write our very own poem. Say back in the country and then river has school been teachers really cared to shape and mold our young minds I don ᵘt see that too much today. Well anyway, I wrote a very profane and intriguing poem. The teacher read it and looked at me and said my goodness. She asked if she could show it to the other teachers and principal; I guess my poem was deep and made a big impact and that was my whole intention. Don't you know she published my poem in the Danville newspaper for all to see and read. I personally love the intellect of poetry.

Well, living in Ringgold in this house we lived in was small and old and cold in the wintertime, but we made it our home. I did find a comfort and a joy of soothing peace to be outside. I was very good with using the axe to chop up firewood to put in that old pot belly stove. This was our only way to heat this house was with firewood. I spent five and six hours cutting up wood using the axe and maul. Countless hours during the winter cutting wood and gazing up at the stars in the sky was my favorite thing to do back then when the time in Virginia was much colder than it is today it seems. I remember when the ground would freeze around October and November and then wouldn't thaw out until around April. I remember when we had to thaw out frozen pipe using 100-Watt light bulb. Don't you know one day it was so cold and my mother wanted to get a fire going in that old potbelly heater and I know it ˈs not safe to do so, but she used gasoline to get the fire started. Well one day she poured a little bit too much gas on that wood; she lit that wood and BOOM, my mother was fine but the explosion burned her eyebrows and eyelashes off.

My mother and my sister Joyce and I just laughed. We had a lot of incidents and accidents like this with close calls. Around about the age of 13,14,15, 16 and 17, I have started to have help problems indescribable. One night I couldn't sleep at all, tossing and turning in my bed. I remember my skin turning very red and I was itching very bad to the point my mother and my sister had to rush me to the hospital at about 2:00 in the morning. Once we arrived at the hospital and the hospital checked me in, they began running every test they could and couldn't find the cause of my burning and my pain, but they could see that my skin was broken out as if I was in hives.

Being rushed to the hospital for itching and pain has started to become a normal occurrence. And remember my dad came to visit us and he brought a hospital bill and said to my mother what's wrong with the boy. He showed us a hospital bill for $160,000 from the hospital. I remember the pain sometimes it would come, sometimes it would go but the pain was very consistent now doing my early to mid-teenage years.

Meanwhile the 9th and 10th grade would prove to be challenging, but with God, and my sister Joyce help I made it through. I would go on to the 11th and 12th grade. Again, in my opinion I have had some of the best teachers in the world. One day the teachers came to me and said that I should take a trade at the Vocational- tech school. I looked at their program and signed up for masonry which would be the best decision.

Going to the vocational school for my masonry trade would be a way for me to take classes in the morning and then take a 11mile ride after lunch from Ringgold VA to Chatham VA for my Vo tech classes. My masonry teacher would be Mr. Womack. Mr. Womack is an amazing man as well as the best teacher I know, he made it his goal to shape and mold us 8 men who was in the class, to be upright men. He introduced us to masonry and how to lay bricks, blocks and stone. How to read blueprints, lay to the line and to level, plumb and straighten Bricks. Masonry is an art that Mr. Womack instilled in us, and I remember when Mr. Womack entered me and my friend Brian into the masonry contest which was going to be held at the Richmond County fair in Richmond VA.

Don't you know that Lieutenant governor Douglas welder was at the fair. Lawrence Douglas Wilder is the first black governor of Virginia from 1990 to 1994. This made the masonry contest more intriguing and fascinating to me come time to compete and there were about 20 of us building a small project that was handed to us to build for the competition. I gave my all and was the first one to finish because we were being judged also on how quickly we finished as well. My friend Brian Brandon is second.

I was so happy because I knew I had won first place in this masonry contest. After the competition I walked out of the hall, and there in the hall was met by the most beautiful girl in the world. She approached me and told me her name then she said you've done an amazing job, but you won't win. I was stunned that she said this to me. Then she slowly walked away gracefully. Then came the ceremony and the trophy awards part. It's like the young lady had told me face to face, I did not win, and I was very devastated. I remember oh so well the long trip back home I cried but, I was happy and at least at peace that one person saw I done good.

That very next day at school Mr. Womack gave me and Brian an award that meant the whole world to the both of us. My teachers made learning fun and interesting. Don't you know that with God's love and grace and mercy I did not miss a day of school my junior and senior year. I was in class everyday my last years of school learning and taking in as much as I can. My mother trusted me to the point that she would let me drive me and my sister to school sometime in the car. Well while trying to finish school, I fell in love with a lovely young lady, and we even made plans to get married. Things began to get serious between us; so serious that this relationship would bring forth my very first child.

So, my first child was born a son. I was there when my son was born, and I even cut the umbilical cord. It seemed to me that in my mind I would be hurting my baby, so the doctor helped me a lot with cutting the umbilical cord. This would be the greatest day of my life. When the nurses cleaned up my child, I remember the nurse handed me my son placing him in my arms I looked at him and smiled, walked over to the window and tell God here is your child Lord use him as you will. Well, my son's mother and I grew apart. I loved her, but her heart was somewhere else and that was OK with me.

I had had my first child, and it was time to buckle down and take care of my baby, I continue to go to doctors, and they run tests after tests and just didn't have a clue as to what was wrong with me, they just knew something not right. was working part time during the summer my junior and senior year of school and then I became full time at this produce supplier in Danville VA. My boss was Mr. Donnie. Mr. Donnie was the owner of the produce company I was working for and was even featured on Forbes magazines as one of the richest men in Virginia Mr. Donnie was a good man and very nice to work for.

I remember being out in the front yard shooting a little hoops on the basketball court, never in my life will I forget while being outside there came a black evil, black smoke like I've never seen before and it was slowly passing by our driveway it was the death Angel.

I prayed to God that if the death Angel had to take one of us to please let it be me. Not my mother nor my sister but me. And my mother came to Joyce and me right in the living room and I'll always remember my mother told us that this house had too much work and repairs to be done on it and that we would be moving. My sister Joyce didn't like that at all and said to my mother "Corey can fix it up". I could tell my sister did not want to move at all and neither did I so many wonderful and great memories happen at this house. We ended up moving from Ringgold VA the county to Danville VA the city. My mother had found a house in the city, and we made the best of it that we could.

Danville VA has a lot of history. It has been featured in a lot of great movies and a lot of movie stars have family in Danville. From Elizabeth Taylor the movie star to NBA players to NFL players. Danville VA is where the first African American race car driver Mr. Wendell Oliver Scott was born and lived. Many might remember the late, great comedian, Richard Pryor made a movie called "grease lightning" about Mr. Wendell Scott's life, a very good movie.

Roundabout this time I was 21 years old I could not for the life of me know why I would stay in so much pain. The doctors knew I was in pain, and they knew I was very sick, but they did not know what the cause of my sickness was. I had learned to cope with severe pain in my body.

I decided to go to social services and file for disability because the pain was making it beyond difficult for me to work. I went into the social service office to file for disability. There was a white lady there at the desk peeling an orange, To the desk and politely said that I would like to apply for disability. The lady looked me up and down and said you want to apply for disability? A politely said yes ma'am. She then handed me a large stack of paper and said here fill this out. After an hour of filling out papers I returned the paperwork to the lady. She took the paperwork and threw it in the trash can right in front of me and said go find you a job.

This broke my heart, and I was very sad, I cannot believe I've been working since I was 15 years old now I am 21 and I'm sick and nobody knows with what. I would try working again as much as I could and just deal with the pain. I answered the ad in the newspaper for a truck driving job for local furniture company. One of my biggest passions is driving. I got the job delivering furniture and I really liked it. This job with the furniture company was a good job. I remember going to the Christmas party with this job and they took us out to a nice steakhouse during the Christmas holiday. I had so much fun at this fantastic restaurant, the atmosphere was superb, and the food was delicious.

Everything seemed to be going well with my job, and I had met a young lady and was spending a lot of my time with her when I'm not working. My sister Joyce had met a man and had become close to this man and his family. My sister Joyce was working and asked me if I could help get the guy she was dating for a job and of course I did without hesitation. He worked with me on the truck delivering and setting up furniture as I was training him. I notice that this guy my sister had chosen to date seems to be very troubled and disturbed within himself. I recall one rainy night we all were awakened by a banging on the door. It was about 2:00 in the morning when I opened the door, and it was Joyce's boyfriend covered in blood. He was on his way to see my sister and encountered a group a boys that he knew and they beat him almost to death but somehow he made it two blocks up the street to our house.

My sister called the police and the ambulance, and she stopped most of the bleeding to help arrive, she nursed him back to health, see he had been cut up very badly and beaten. When the police came, he would not tell who had done this to him. Well, a little more time went by, and my sister ended up marrying him and I family didn't think this was such a good idea based on his history with us. This guy had a very bad temper and was in an unruly fashion and display voguer language. I was staying at a very close lady friend apartment just working when I can and battling this unknown pain over my body. I was 24 years old, and my sister was 22 years old. One day while visiting over at my mother*s house, where we all used to live, my mother said that my sister had brought her a cup of soup by the laundromat, and this was on a Saturday. Sunday had come and nobody had heard from my sister, but I thought it was no big deal. Well, Monday came, and all this took place during the month of August, and the afternoon had come. The phone rang around 2:00 in the afternoon. It was the Community College, and I was the one who answered the phone. The lady was so nice and polite and said to me that my sister did not show up for class that day. It bothered me but I thought nothing of it really. What really bothered me was when my sister Joyce job called and said that Joyce did not show up for work that day.

My heart hit my stomach so hard because this was out of my sister's character now. Then I became very worried. See after a few months of being married to this guy my sister separated from him because he was doing drugs very heavy as we found out. And from this marriage to this guy my sister had a very beautiful baby boy that was about 7 months old at this point.

My family and I had not seen or heard from my sister in days. I decided to go to her apartment and my friend who I was staying with also went with me, as well and she was also a friend of my sister too. My friend and I got to the apartment, and I went up to the door and knocked, but there was no answer at all, so I continued to knock even louder. I had become very afraid for my sister's safety, and I banged on that door and banged and banged so hard I never stopped banging for about 5 to 10 minutes. Just as I had got tired of banging and knocking, I turn my back and began to walk away, and all of a sudden I heard a baby crying in that apartment.

I mean it was a lot of commotion going on all over the apartment but, I specifically heard a baby crying coming from my sister's door to her apartment. I asked my friend did she heard a baby crying and she replied yes, I hear a baby crying also. Don't you know I told my friend that I'm not going anywhere. I had a flip phone, so I remember just as if it was yesterday, I flipped my phone open and dial 911. When I called 911, I told the police on the other line that there is a baby crying in my sister's house and I can't get my sister to come to the door they had traced the phone call and knew exactly where I was at, and they told me that they would be right over.

So, three police cars pulled up and when the police came, I showed them which apartment and I told them to put their ear up to the door and they did and said I hear a baby in there. The police asked me where is our mother and father. I got very busy on the phone calling everybody because I felt in my soul that something was not right. The police had got in touch with the maintenance man who had keys to the apartment and tell him to get over there. The police also asked me where was our mother and I replied she's at work and the officer told me to go get her. With all that was unfolding, the pain that I had lived with from when I was a teenager up until now has become so drastically worse in my body. I could not deal with what was unfolding in front of me. This was turning into the worst day of my life. At this point a very cold and lifeless chill was going all over my body.

I had done as the police had requested, and rushed to my mother's job and I told my mother that she needed to get to my sister's apartment the police needed her there. I had also called my daddy and my other brothers and sisters and told them what was going on. At this time my family had assembled all around the apartment and we were waiting on the maintenance man to get there with the keys. The Danville police did not know what to expect so they went in with their guns drawn once the maintenance man opened the door and they pushed him out the way.

Nothing in this world can prepare a human being for the drastic ungodly scene that was playing out. There was a crowd that had gathered at this point about 100 to 200 people had gathered. Next, they entered that apartment, and they found the baby, my nephew crawling around on the floor within a lot of fluids and liquids. They made their way to the bedroom, banged on the door and then knocked the door down where they found my sister on the bed with a gunshot wound to the head. My daddy said that we would find her husband and make him pay, but the police said there is no need to find him because he's in the bedroom also dead with a self-inflicted gunshot wound to the head also. So sadly, I remember being numb from the top of my head to the bottom of my feet, numb! The police started putting up their crime scene tape and that just made me very furious, as they would put their tape up in a very deep anger, I would rip it down. I was so angry that I didn't want to live, I wanted to die. Why it couldn't have been me was the thought going through my head. When they brought my sister's baby, my nephew out, my sister that is older than me took the baby from the police officer and rushed him to the hospital. I remember seeing him pass right by in front of me, his lips were purple, his face was turning blue. I could not believe what was happening. How could the act of one person Cause so much hurt and pain for so many people. After maybe an hour the police had finished their investigation they asked me questions, they asked other people questions then they allowed us to go in and see my sister's body. It hurts me to even think about it now, because I remember seeing my daddy and my mother and my brothers and sisters as they came out that apartment door crying. I could not bear to see my sister, so I did not go back in to see her body. I was the only one that did not see her. My mother who was close to Joyce and me, when she came out, she looked at me crying and said that's not Joyce, that's not our Joyce. She looked at me and said remember her the way she was.

All our life, Joyce and I agreed that we will go to see God our creator and lover of our life together. When my older sister went to college and my mother worked from sunup to sundown, all Joyce and I had was each other. We made the best out of every situation and we've done it with a smile oh not face. We were not picky or choosy. We were very content with whatever came our way. Now the only friend that I ever had is gone. Don't you know for the first time in my whole entire life I did not want to live. I was battling A chronic gruesome pain all in my body and now I have lost the only friend I ever had in my life I remember hearing the police chief asking my mother "do you want us to get him some help", talking about me, and maybe I should have got the help that I needed. I thought about when I seen that death Angel come down the road on state route 729 where we lived and moved from and just kept asking the question why. After sitting there at that apt that night with everybody crying and so much commotion going on, I reasoned within myself and said that I must live for my sister Joyce and for my nephew.

My mother and my older sister who went to college, took my nephew and raised him which most definitely was a disturbing struggle and quite understandable being that my nephew was just six months old when this matter happened and had to grow up with no mother nor father. I tried my very best to work and do the best that I could after the loss of my sister. I got a job building tires on the U-2 machine for a well-known tire and rubber company, the number one in the world. This companybuilt tires for all vehicles but my job was building tires for the Air Force for airplanes and aircraft. During this time, I was living at home with my mother and trying to cope with what had happened I was raised in the church to love honor and respect God and I did, but my life was going on a downward spiral.

Then I ended up dating my high school sweetheart and we were planning to get married, but I just couldn't get my life together at this point. Building the tires was very hard work, I worked 12 hours shifts from 7:00 PM till 7:00 AM honestly, I don't know how I did this job. While dating and preparing to get married, my high school sweetheart and I had a baby, and the baby was a girl my second child. While being overjoyed with having my second child and my very first baby girl,

I was very excited, but I also had come to a breaking point in my life and just couldn't get my life together. I was young and had no sense of direction and now I have two children that I love and must take care of. At just 22 years old my sister and best friend were no longer there for me I had an empty feeling in my life. A few years after my daughter was born and the relationship was going nowhere between her mother and I, my only choice, I thought, was to leave Danville to find a new life and a new job. My friend that I have been staying with, she was tired of Danville VA as well and wanted to go with me, and I had no idea where I was going. All I know is that this was going to be my very first time having to live away from family and I had no friends on top of staying sick all the time. My sickness and pain transgressed more and more as I tried to work, and I couldn't, and we ended up being homeless. I would use my masonry skills to make some money from time to time as well, but laying brick and block is a very strenuous job. After being away from Danville VA for a long while, I told my friend that it was time to go back home and she agreed.

I then called back to my mother's house to find out that they had been worried about me and concerned for me. The first person that I talked to was my older sister, and the first thing she told me was that my other sister had passed away. I was in shock yet again, now I have two sisters gone. I moved back to my mother's house and my friend moved back to her family's house. While I was gone from Danville VA there was a court date and I had failed to appear, which in legal terms is called a failure to appear which is automatically jail time. I went to the court to turn myself in and this was on a Friday, which means that I would not see a judge until Monday morning. When I went to the court to turn myself in, they told me that I missed my court date and that they would have to hold me until Monday till I see the judge.

There was a lady deputy who took me and put me in a holding cell I walked into that holding cell and there was a black man in there, just him and me. This guy was about 6 feet tall and five inches, a very big robust guy, with wild looking hair and sweating and blood all over his T-shirt. Yes, this guy had blood all over his shirt and jeans and I was very afraid. I kept my eyes on him, and he was acting as if he didn't want me near him. Sweat was just running from his face as he kept staring at me out of the corner of his eye and mumbling to himself very wild looking guy.

After about 30 minutes of this, a man deputy came and opened the cell door and told me to come out and I did. This deputy asked another deputy who was standing there, he said in a very loud voice who put this man in this cell. I can tell he was very mad he said, "you can't put him in there with this man, this man has killed three people today", wow! Don't you know this killer looked at me out of the corner of his eyes with fear like he was afraid of me, when I was the one afraid of him. I had never had anyone look at me with such fear in their eyes except for one time when my friend and I were living out of town. I remember I go to the store to buy some cookies and chips and then a black guy came in with a gun. I froze, because I was very afraid. this guy started to point the gun at the man behind the register and midway he paused, he turns around completely at me with great fear, but I'm the one who's afraid. This guy with the gun his eyes became very big, and he started shaking and saying out loud "I see something, I see something in you, I see something around you, and this guy dropped his gun and ran fast as he could. Well about 5 minutes had gone by and they had arrested the man, we all had to give a statement and I told the police that I don't know what was going on. Go back to when I first got locked up in jail, so the deputy put me in the population cell with ten other men and the deputy gave me a blanket and a mat to sleep on, because I had to sleep on the floor. Don't you know, one of the men took my blanket from under my arms, and I'll never forget he made my bed up for me right down on the floor. One of the other prisoners said, "let that man make his own bed up". The man making up my bed said "no", he said we belong here, but this man doesn't.

I made it through the weekend which seems like a forever. When that Monday morning came, I've seen the judge and told him that I failed to appear because I was out of town and was unaware of a court date and the judge let me go free. I then got other jobs trying to work still and do the best that I can in spite of the pain all over my body. I had to learn how to smile and hurt at the same time.

One day when I just thinking, I recall telling God when I was 16 years old that if I had to suffer in this life then it would be worth it to live pain free with him forever. I recall in the Bible Job the 14th chapter and the first verse tell us that man that is born of a woman is of a few days and full of trouble. I also recall in the the Bible psalms 23rd chapter and 4th verse say yea though I walk through the valley of the shadows of death I will fear no evil: for thou art with me: they rod and staff they comfort me. And living in this world is the valley of the shadows of death we live in every day, and I have seen the death, Angel.

Well, I thank God for my mother who told me to try the spirit and make sure it's of God, and at this point in my life I just continue to work in excruciating pain to pay my child support. I have started to pray more and read God's word more as I did more and more of this God made himself more and more plain to me.

My mother told me one day to pray and God will send me somebody. So, I started to do just like she's saying, and I pray for a mate and told God that I was willing to wait no matter how long it takes. I pray as I always do, with a sincere heart and with all humility and humbleness. I made-up in my mind that I would have no other God in my life; no money, clothes, house, family, nothing's come before God in my life. I was baptized by God's own spirit and had no malice nor black matter in my heart, I was drawing closer than ever to God each day.

While waiting on God I also knew I had to look as well so I decided to go to the library and get on the computer. I had wanted to find me a new place to live with good jobs, and good homes and better opportunities, so when I got to the library, they assigned me a computer; don't you know I was sitting right beside this lady that had rollers in her hair and she had on scrubs clothing. scrubs are clothing for the medical profession. While sitting next to this lady the worst case of being uneasy hit me. I had never felt like this in my entire life, I couldn't focus on what I was doing so I just got up off the computer and began to leave. I had got about 20 feet away and don't you know I stopped right there in my tracks because I heard a voice! Don't you know this voice said to me, "this is your wife". I turned around and went right back to that same computer and it was still available. So, I pretended to be looking up stuff as I kept looking at this lady out of the corner of my eye.

I've then asked the lady, "are you married"? "No", she replied. With a tremble in my voice and shaking in my heart, I took a chance and asked her, "can I get your number"? She seemed to be frustrated and looked at me and said, "you don't want to talk to me", but still she gave me her number. In turn I gave her my number and at this point I said, "my name is Corey" and she said, "my name is Sharon". I looked at her and smiled and she seemed to be very depressed. Very slowly I got up and she got up as well. We both have park up on the top deck of the library in the parking garage. I went to my car, and she went to her van that she had drove and I watched her leave. I could not believe

God had spoken to me and told me that this woman is my wife.

I waited for her to call me. I didn't want to call her because I didn't know if she would be busy or something. Around about 6:00 PM she called me, and we began to conversate. She told me about her family, and I told her about my family, and she told me that she had children, I told her I have a boy and a girl as well. Sharon said to me that she has five small children, this is the reason she said you don't want to talk to me. she thought because she had five children that no man would want to talk to her with small children and that was not the case with me.

Well, we talked more and got to know each other better over the weekend and then came Monday morning we went to the courthouse and got married. Sharon told me that she was a minister, and i told her that I was a child of GOD and had been for a long time. Sharon was also in the United States Navy and a Registered Nurse. Sharon and her children had gotten to know me the very first week we were together, and I got to know them. Sharon and I found out that we were soulmates and would be best friends.

Soon after we were married and the children got to know me, I asked Sharon what's the plan for our life, being in the military, Sharon and her children had lived in many places. She told me that she was in the library looking for a new start and a new state to settle down in. So, we went back to the library together and looked for a place that we would both like to live. she told me that she had a deep love and passion for the American Indians, and I expressed to her that I did also. I remember starting out our relationship, I would just love to gaze into her beautiful eyes, brown eyes. I would love to hear my wife just talk and just to be close to her gave me the calmest feeling I ever had.

Just like my mother had told me God would send me somebody, and I would thank God for being so good and blessing me with the best gift I could ever receive, the gift to love unconditionally. The Bible says he who finds a wife findeth a good thing, and obtaineth favor of the Lord.

Women are the most precious thing on this planet. Women are a gift from God. So, after a long thought and us praying together and doing our research we agreed to move out West to Arizona. This means we both will have to leave our families and friends in Danville VA and move over 2700 miles to the West Coast. Sharon was in the Navy and a nurse she had gotten a job at the hospital on the Apache reservation with public health services. The hospital had housing for us, and this is where we moved to as a family.

So, Sharon had three girls and two boys who were very young.

When we got to the reservation, we enrolled them in school. So, we packed up everything in Virginia, and she asked me, "do you think my van will make it to Arizona" and I replied, "with God's help we will make it". I drove that van from Danville VA to White River Arizona just me and my beautiful wife and our five children. This would be my first time and Sharon and her children's first time also going to the West Coast. For three days I drove that van day and night, we stopped for gas and snacks, and we took in all the sights along the way and when we made stops. Well, when we get to the reservation and get settled in our house we would shop at the same stores as the Native Americans and on Sundays we would go to church and worship with the American Indians. They see the deep love and compassion my wife had for everyone she treated at the hospital on the reservation. Our kids became friends with their kids at school and everything. I remember Sharon told me about her past relationships and marriages and she was straightforward and honest all the time, she had never been in love her entire life. As for myself I thank God that he planted the seed of love in me when I was very young. I love Sharon in the way God first created and ordained that love between a man and a woman. As a man I would do what I had to for

Sharon, my wife and our five children. I would drive from White River to Pinetop and go lay bricks and block in a development that was being developed. We lived and worked on this reservation with the Apache Indians for more than two years.

We preached and lead people to Christ on the reservation. Every morning my wife would put on her nursing scrubs, that I would have already cleaned and pressed for her to go to work. I would drive my wife to work and then I would take the children to school every morning. We would tell each other that we love each other and give a soft, gentle warm kiss on the lips and a big tight hug every day. One day after work I had picked up Sharon and she got in the van, and she looked at me and could tell that I was in some very excruciating pain because I was holding the right side of my stomach. I told her that I had been in some serious pain ever since I was a teenager, and the doctors did not know what it was. Then she expressed to me that she herself had been having headaches ever since she was a little girl, and no one knew what it was. well, we had lived with the Apache Indians in their housing, and it was wonderful, but Sharon wanted us to get a home and I agreed. Many wonderful and amazing things happened on the Apache reservation, and they hated to see us move but they were happy for us and even expressed to me that my family and I had a home forever. We were a part of the Apache family forever. We searched around and found a home that we liked in the phoenix valley. Sharon and I prayed all the time when she goes to work and I go to work we talked on the phone all the time, it's like we didn't want to be apart from one another and she had that loving protective spirit that God gave her as well. And when we were together, we laughed all the time just making each other happy. After finding the house I let her pick it. I remember she said, "Corey I want this house". Don't you know that I touched and prayed on that house and the next day the landlord said "when can you guys move in" Sharon was so shocked. This house had 6 bedrooms, 4 bathrooms and was only a month otd. This was one of the most beautiful houses we had ever seen, and we know God always provides and make a way and give HIS best to HIS children. And we would always make the 3-hour trip up the mountain to the Apache reservation for church and revivals. Well, I would be driving, and my beautiful, darling wife would be holding my hand and looking at me smiling and I would be looking at her glowing. My adorable wife Sharon also wrote a book about her own autobiography and the title of the book is called "on deadly ground". This book is a very good read, and I would recommend it to anybody. She also wrote a book about nursing and a book about the American Indians, yes, yes, yes, my wife is very smart and the best nurse in the world in my opinion. I love my wife Sharon with all my heart and our five children.

So, at this point in my life, it was becoming more and more clearly why God had placed Sharon and I to live in the phoenix valley and had moved us from the White River mountains. Sharon is GODs child, and I knew this from the start, and I remember all so well how we worked together to help all people no matter what color, ethnic background, lifestyle no matter we helped and loved people.

One day while taking Sharon to work we were passing through downtown phoenix, and everybody knows what the traffic is like downtown in phoenix, it is very crazy, they drive fast it's a mess. Well, I was driving taking my wife to work and all of a sudden Sharon yelled out "stop the car" ! Don't you know that before I could stop that car she had jumped out and sheltered this kid from being hit by that crazy speeding traffic. She put her body to the surrounding this kid.

So, she took this kid by the hand, it was a white boy about 16 years old and she put him in the car in the back seat. this kid was completely blind, and he had his walking stick and he told us that he missed the bus on his way to the school for the blind. So, we Google the school and got him there safely, we got to witness to this young man about God and he was so happy and glad that Sharon had saved his life, because just two blocks away we had seen a pickup truck take off from the red light and hit a guy on his bicycle.

This is what my wife Sharon and I done every day on a regular basis. We have heard people from all walks of life and from all over the world. It was a hot July day, and the temperatures were high as you can imagine. I remember the temperature being 112 degrees this day. We were going into the convenience store to get us a cold drink, Sharon loved her drink with lots of ice from the fountain drinks. While walking up to the door, and Sharon walking right behind me, we had gotten to the front door of the store and notice this Asian family was coming out of the door. There was an elderly lady in the family, and she began to fall and as she was falling, she was reaching for me and I caught her in my arms, thank God almighty that we were there, I caught her in my arms and Sharon broke out in nurse mode right then and right there and began to assess the lady, we found out she was dehydrated.

The elderly Asian lady was the mother of the son of the couple, and they were so overjoyed that we were there to help his mother. There was another time I remember it was a Monday, we were on our way to work, and we needed some gas, so I pulled up to the gas station which was very busy with people going in and out. This time it was in August and the temperature was over 100 degrees. There was this young girl at the pump with the hood of her car up. So, Sharon and I walked over to see how we might help her this young lady was Hispanic and pregnant. See people don't understand that love is kind and understanding and patience. Sharon and I put all three into action with this young lady because we took the time to understand that she spoke no English, and we didn't speak much Spanish. This young lady made it very plain for us to understand that her car would not start, and she was on her way to the hospital to deliver her baby. So, I took jumper cables out of the trunk and connected them to her battery and the car started for this young lady, she was so happy and overjoyed, and she began to cry and gave us a hug. I let the hood down on her car and she drove on to the hospital. I could not understand for the life of me, all the men around going in and out of the store nobody stopped to help her, only Sharon and me. That very next day in that afternoon, we went to the grocery store to get food for dinner for our family. While pulling up at the grocery store, we noticed a pickup truck and the hood was up on it as well. So, we pulled over to see if we could be of some assistance.

There was an elderly Hispanic man and his son. The man's spoke no English, but his young son spoke English very good and translated to his father as we asked, "what was the problem with the truck". His son told us that the truck would not start because the battery was dead. So, Sharon looked at me and said, "how much is a battery". From my experience of buying an automotive battery, down through the years for cars and trucks of my own, I knew that a battery would run about $75 dollars. Don't you know that $75 was all the money that we had between us and that's what we were going to use to buy food for our family. Sharon looked at me and I looked at her and the two of us began to laugh and smile. I went into my pocket and pulled out that $75 and handed it to the gentleman and told his son to tell him that we were helping him to get a new battery. This elderly Hispanic man broke out in tears of joy just crying they both were so happy. Me and Sharon was so happy because this gave us a chance to find Stuff at home to put together to make a meal and God provided and we had plenty to eat, and God's word plainly tells us man shall not live by bread alone. Sharon and I always enjoyed cooking every day and all the time. This is what made us both so very happy. We just loved each other so much till it was unbelievable, because you didn't see, and you cannot find this kind of love anywhere on the planet, and it was rare if you did find it. It became so very clear that the seed of love had been planted in both our hearts and souls by God himself. So, after praying and talking it over with each other we realize that it was time that we start our own church and lead as many to Christ that we could. I told Sharon that the name of our church would become The Rose of Sharon House of prayer. She really liked the name of our church home. Now we have a name for our church, but I want my church to be different and abide by the laws of this land and pay its taxes. Already I noticed we were starting out different from other religious churches or groups or whatever you want to call them., and we have family meetings regularly with the children and I and Sharon. I got my family together and told them what I was about to do, I told them that our church would be paying its taxes and that

I would need to get my EIN number from the IRS. That's the Employer Identification number, that the IRS issues your company or business.

While we were all together and in our family meeting, called the IRS and I put my phone on speaker so Sharon and the kids could be a part of what was going on. So, I called the IRS, and a very lovely lady answered the phone and said "hello". I said "hello" I told her that I was starting my church and that I want my church to pay its taxes and that I wanted to get my EIN number. The young lady took my information and then gave me my new EIN number. I was so happy and thrilled. Don't you know that this wonderful lady said, after she had given me my number, "Sir I don't know you, but wherever your church is I will fly out to your church wherever it's at". My wife Sharon and all the children looked at me in amazement.

They said wow the spirit of God travels through the phone just like that. And by any chance if that young lady is reading My Autobiography, please by all means reach out and contact me for the location of my church we would love to have you come visit and thank you. Children of GOD needs to come together in times like these. So, Sharon and I spent all our time devoted to God and our children and working and being a servant to the public that we encountered every day not just preaching God's word but living it also to the best of our ability.

I would always enjoy working in the hospitals and nursing homes alongside my wife Sharon, she would be doing the nursing part, and I would be running the maintenance and cleaning. I remember one patient my lovely wife was taking care of was a 14-year-old Hispanic girl. This young lady was in a very drastic and dire situation, see she was young and while hanging out with her friends in the car with her "so-called friends", they were involved in a very serious car accident.

There was four of them and three passed away but thank God this young lady survived the accident. The problem is now she was wounded very badly. Sharon treated her day after day. The girl's mother and father were with her every day and night they're at the hospital every day. Sharon would take her stuffed animal to this young lady. She just cried all the time and told Sharon that she just wanted to be like the other kids.

So, she was wounded so badly that her intestines were on the outside of her body. Well one night while at home Sharon said to me, I know if you pray for her, she will be healed. Sharon had seen for years as well as the children, that my relationship with God is like nothing they had ever seen before. Well, I went down on my knees and prayed for this young lady, and don't you know that seven days went by, and she recovered from her wounds. The doctors were able to remove the colostomy bag and she was completely ready to go back to school with her friends when the doctors told her plainly that she would never be the same again and she could never go to school again in her condition. Her mother and father did not know what to say and they just shed tears of joy and kept thanking us for taking care of their daughter. This was an amazing day. God is so very good.

Like I said before, Sharon and I would be working in nursing homes and hospitals together. I would do the maintenance of the building and the cleaning. Sharon Would be doing nursing as an assistant director of nursing (ADON) and director of nursing (DON) and even be the administrator of a facility sometimes. Yes, Sharon is the best nurse there is because of her deep love and passion and belief for everybody. This was what kept her going daily. The real work, success and effectiveness of my wife Sharon, can be determined and seen from all my wife accomplishments and awards and letters and accolade after accolade, her life speaks for itself. She gave many speaking engagements and countless services and revivals. My wife and I worked together and was very happy, but my pain that I 've had, seemed like my whole life kept getting worse and I noticed that my darling wife Sharon headaches kept getting worse.

Not only am I a brick Mason, and not only did I work with my wife in the healthcare industry, but I also enjoy serving the public through the hotel industry. I learned a long time ago how to clean rooms, make beds etc... I remember one day while working in this hotel which happens to be one of the best hotels to stay with, I woke up and went to work like I always have done. On this day I arrived at work and one of my favorite things to do was to go to the top floor using the elevator and look out over phoenix city.

I walked up to the elevator and notice that it was coming down from the top floor as I'm standing there waiting for the elevator to get down, I noticed four men walked up to the elevator door and they assault salt rifles strapped to their backs. There were two black guys and two white guys who we're wearing sunglasses and in suits. This was very unusual and frightening for me because I had never seen anything like this before. When the elevator opened there came out beautiful African ladies. People were going up and bowing down to the one in the center of the group. I have never seen anything like this in my entire life. Then the one in the middle walked up to me and stood face to face and toe to toe with me, and she was very beautiful. She spoke some words and they were beautiful words in French, but I did not understand. See I have studied some French before, and the other four women giggled and laughed as the lady slowly walked away from me. Never will I forget one of the women in the group walked up to me and said the queen said, "you are a beautiful black man". I was in complete shock and numb.

A real queen from Africa spoke to me directly in my face! I had a great day at work that day and couldn't wait to tell my wife Sharon what had happened to me. Don't you know I watched the group get in a Pearl color Rolls Royce, which is my dream car, and that Rolls Royce was surrounded by 8 black SUV. I stood there in the window of that hotel and watched them drive away, then I went to the front desk and asked why they didn't tell me that we had guests at this hotel. They laughed and said, "Corey, we thought you knew the queen was coming today". I made it home that afternoon after work and told Sharon that a real African queen spoke to me, and I could see that she really didn't believe me, because we played around all the time, and like most women, she googled everything. Sharon got on her phone and googled and yes it was all over the news that an African queen has a treaty with the United States and came to visit to check on her people who are working here in America for a period. So, then Sharon believed me and knew that I was real at this point. I told her what the queen said to me, and Sharon agreed and said yes you are a beautiful black man. As time went on day by day, I notice my pain in my right side getting worse and worse, and not only that my beautiful lovely wife, she had tried her best to keep her headache pain from me but I knew something was not right.

As our ministry grew so did our faith and love for God. Sharon used her magnificent nursing skills to help heal people with God's love and guidance, and I was still preaching and living so God can use me. I can tell you this, come a little over a year after being married, Sharon's mother gets sick and ultimately pass away. She was a very beautiful lady inside and out with a heart of gold. This would be one of the worst days of my wife's life. I thank God that I was there to support and help my wife get through this life changing ordeal. Sharons mother really loved and cared for me as well as her son-in-law. And I was so pleased to have her as my mother-in-law.

I remember one day when I got off work at the hotel I was going home, and I was very hungry. I cannot make it home I have got to get me something to eat. So, on my way home I stopped by my favorite restaurant, Golden Corral. I was so happy to be pulling up at this place. I got out of the car and was walking up to the door, and I noticed that there were about seven or eight people coming up behind me and I thought that I would hold the door open for them because I like being courteous and kind to people. Well as I got to the door, I noticed a very large crowd of people coming to leave the restaurant.

Ok, I would hold the door open for the group to come out as well. I took the door handle and opened the door for the first person and that was an elderly lady. This lady walked up to me and stood face to face with me and looked at me and smiled. As she looked at me and smiled, she said "you are going to heaven". Don't you know that's not all she said to me. She said a whole lot of things to me that she could not possibly have known. She was telling me stuff that I had done a long time ago. God had revealed to her in that instant things about me. This white lady was telling me stuff about me and stuff that happened to me that I had forgot all about. She softly touched my face and walked away. Then as I continue to hold the door open for the rest of the group, a man came up to me and smiled and said that they were celebrating his mother 98 birthday. Everyone in the group looked at me as if they were seeing a ghost.

I was so happy that God used this lady at her age to let people know that I am his child. After I ate, I was so excited to go home and tell my wife what had happened to me. So, when I got home, I told Sharon what happened, she said "yes the lady is right you are going to heaven". My wife Sharon and I had real love. Equally yoked with God true love not like this deceitful mess like this world considered Love. My lovely wife devoted her life and time, and I did as well to treating and caring for people on a professional level with love and passion, that's undeniably plain to see. So, we lived on the West Coast for many years and my wife, and I talked about maybe moving back to the East Coast for a little while. We decided to move, and we found a very nice little house for our family in Augusta GA. Sharon had gotten a job as a director of nursing at a nursing home and she really loved the residence there. She treated and cared for the residents with the utmost respect. I remember one day my wife and I went out to go get some food for us and the children; while going down the road I noticed a car had flipped over on its rooftop there were young kids, four of them on the ground. What does my wife do when we pull up on a scene like this as always jump out the car and assist the children. We were in the right place at the right time because the children were hurt badly with broken bones and things of that nature.

We found out that they had stolen a Mercedes Benz and was speeding and fost control, that's what happened, and the oldest one was 16 years old. Just babies.

At this point in my life, I have become more and more concerned with the pains that I have been dealing with since I was a teenager. I am noticing that my lovely wife has headaches more consistently now. I don't know what to do. I gaze into her eyes and can see love and joy. Not just any love and joy, but the joy she has for me is the joy of the Lord God and there will be few that will ever find this kind of love and joy and peace that passes all understanding. I am just as much in love with my wife as she is with me. As a matter of fact, the only disagreement that we have is about who loves who more and they can last a long time but smiling all the time at each other.

One night while lying in bed, because we both were tired, then noticed it was raining very hard and storming badly outside, and this was about midnight. Don't you know my wife sat up in the bed and said "listen". I couldn't believe my ears it sounded like a freight train was coming through the house. I was very afraid, but I had to be strong for my wife. Now the nursing home where she worked was just one mile down the road from the house, we were living in. The roaring of the train sound got louder and louder as the train was coming through our living room and suddenly maybe in one or two minutes it stopped.

Sharon and I had feared the worst. I will never forget Sharon looked at me and told me to take her to the nursing home so she could check on her residence. Don't you know right after she said that her cell phone rang, and we looked at each other.

We knew what had happened. She answered her phone, and we feared the worst. A tornado hit the nursing home and it was a big tornado. As quickly as I could, I drove Sharon to the nursing home and when we pulled up, I could not believe my eyes. This nursing home took a direct hit from this tornado that had just gone right over our house. Don't you know that the King James holy Bible: John 15-chapter 13 verse say "greater love has no man than this, that a man lay down his life for his friends. This will prove to be my wife Sharon the greatest challenge ever.

you see I have no problem with people getting their degrees and higher learning that's all fine and dandy, but that's all-man knowledge, and as a minister of God my darling wife and I both knew that only wisdom from God would get her through this disaster. When I pulled up to this nursing facility the first thing we did when we arrived was pray that everyone was OK first, then we hugged and kissed each other. I looked my wife in the eyes, and I told her that "you got this", I can only say that it was a miracle that not one person was killed. The roof was going and some of the walls were gone as well, you could plainly see the outline of the tornadoes path. So proud of my wife for how she went to work hard and just like a soldier on the battlefield. Ambulance after ambulance, car after car. They even brought in buses after buses pulling up to transport the residence from Ground Zero to other hospitals and nursing homes close by. My wife had to assess every resident and their record had to follow them to whichever hospital or nursing home they were moving to. Nothing in my wife's life has or could ever have prepared her for this disaster. I've watched her work tirelessly moving each resident one at a time, eventually the news people showed up. My amazing wife gave her all to take care of everybody, and I say amazing because that's what all the police and paramedic and firefighters all said about her actions, she was amazing to take charge because she was the DON.

Take charge and calm the nurses that were working that night Shandon done all this and so much more while being sick with that very severe headache. At this point I could see plan and clear God's purpose and planning for us to move to Augusta GA. not many men nor women can let God use them to do a job like this. Totally amazing and I witnessed it all! So, amazing and miraculous things happen to us, and for us in Augusta GA.

Sharon had an amazing spirit about connecting with people. I took her to check on her patients that were moved to other nursing homes and hospitals. While sitting in the car she was in the hospital visiting her residence. I noticed cars coming in at a very fast pace and speeding in the entrance and people got out of the vehicles and ran inside going to the emergency room. Not long after that, maybe in a 30-minute Timeline, I noticed men and women coming out of the hospital Mad and hitting the trash cans and very upset and crying and screaming. This family had just lost their grandmother, and then Sharon was coming out of the hospital. She seen what was going on and started to hug the family and calmed them down.

On November the 9th was the day Sharon was scheduled to have surgery on her skull and brain. As we get closer and closer to the date, I would have an Angel visit me in my spirit and Sharon would have angels visit her in her spirit as well. Just like in psalm the 91st chapter and the 11th verse it tells us "For HE shall give HIS angels charge over thee to keep thee in all thy ways".

I wanted Sharon to wait until after the holidays came to have this surgery done, but how selfish of me. I just didn't like the odds of the survival rate from this type of surgery. The Chiari malformation odds by this doctor were 50/50. I continue to take my darling lovely wife to her appointment. I would cook for my wife whatever she wanted in this world to eat and clean the house and take care of the children, she didn't have to do anything. I love my wife and I praise God every day of my life for giving me the best that he has. We have always been best friends from day one. We have always respected each other from day one and never crossed the respectful line. We have always taken care of each other from day one. Love is more essential than food, water, and even a place to live.

Real true love come from God, because of God. The Bible plainly tells us John the 15th chapter and 13th verse "greater love have no man than this that a man lay down his life for his friends". My beautiful darling wife perform this every day. I performed it as well and still do. People can read and quote scripture and never understand or know what it means.

I thank God, that he is God and nothing like man. I am so happy to know that when this life in this body is over, I can be with my creator and take nothing out of this world but memories of people I've tried to help, people that I did help and wished I could help. One thing my darling wife Sharon and I did was reflect every day, every minute and every second we just reflect and reminisce on atl we had been through together. This gave us peace while waiting and praying for this operation to be a successful one. I can see the fear in her eyes, I can see the hesitation, but I also can see that love and joy that my wife has everywhere she put her feet.

The entire week leading up to her operation we just would reminisce and think and laugh and play and talk about all the wonderful things God had ordained us to do and took us through. One day while reminiscing I asked my wife I said remember when we were on the reservation. This Sunday we had went to visit and worship with the American Indian, and they had told my wife Sharon that they wanted their grandmother to be healed. So about 20 of them came to our house and had a bottle of oil and asked if I would pray for God's blessing on the oil. I prayed over this oil and ask God's blessings and he blessed it, and they took it home and then anointed their grandmother. They anointed the walls of the house and car and everywhere. Well, the grandmother had been bedridden for over five years, she could not use her legs or move to get out of bed in over five years. Don't you know there is healing in Gods spirit.

All of this took place on a Sunday afternoon, and don't you know next Monday morning their grandmother was up washing dishes and cleaning up the house. God is so good, and this is the God that Sharon and I serve every day of our life. The children and grandchildren could do nothing but cry with tears of joy and praising God. I want the entire world to know that the Hispanic nation, the Apache nation, the Cherokee Nation, the Navajo Nation, the wasaja Nation and the oriental nation, and the African nation and all nations abroad, will forever and always be our brothers and sisters and friends who we love.

I mean we talk and talk from 5:00 in the morning when we get up to 12 midnight when we went to bed just reminiscing together. Not boasting or bragging on anything we've ever done to help anybody but being used by God. We were so thankful we could think about the hundreds and thousands and thousands of people we had helped and continue to help today not doing anything looking for a reward or pay, but doing everything to help our brother and our sister which means the world to us. Every single living human being on this planet is special to the creator and to know what love is, real love, not as the entertainers and elites and principalities in high places consider love, but GOD considers love, my wife and I will lay down our life and do it with a smile for anybody. To love somebody that hates your very existence is what love is all about. I mean look at the news and search the Internet there is murder and mass killings every day all over this world and you cannot find two people that can get along anywhere so tell me again who knows what love is, I will wait...............

Not only did we help so many people I thank God that after my nephew had lost mother and his father, that my wife Sharon had become close friends with him and could talk to him and help him. See in high school the children would pick on him for so long and he knew not why they were picking on him. Some kids are just evil as we all know, And I remember when he called from Danville VA to Arizona and asked me what happened to his mother, and I was in shock that they did not tell him what had happened. I guess my mother was just trying to keep it away from him, maybe like pulling a Band-Aid from a bruise or something. So, while on the phone with my nephew, I looked at Sharon and I said, "they didn't tell him what happened to his mother and father". I said a quick prayer and began to tell him what had happened, and he seemed not to be too much bothered but I could tell it hurt him I also knew that he was a strong man and could take it and had to know what had happened to his mother and father. This was one of the most difficult things in my life to do was to tell him this dreadful God-awful news. This is a lot for a very young man to deal with or anybody for that matter. It was a complete total struggle for my mother to single handedly raise him by herself with my sister's help, but she did. I cannot wait to read his autobiography; it's going to be a book to remember.

Well November the 8 that evening I ventured out to buy my wife something special to take with her to the hospital for her surgery. I found the most beautiful water globe with the Angel inside. It was special to me for her. Sharon loves to hug her husband and spend as much quality time as she can with him. I remember that night we had hungry Howie's pizza and I remember she wanted me to shave the back of her head and get it ready for surgery. November the 8th 2013 seems like I was living in a total eclipse. It will always remain the strangest day of my life.

I have found the masterpiece in my wife, and she has found her masterpiece within me. Love is a wonderful and amazing thing. love is so kind and sweet and patience is love, waiting is love, understanding and not jumping to conclusions is love. After shaving my wife head and getting it the way, she wanted, we continue to laugh and talk and enjoy each other 's company and continue reminiscing about the good old times we had and how GOD used us for HIS will. I told Sharon do she recall how God used her one day on the reservation. It was a Saturday night to remember. That whole entire day, Sharon had been saying her hands were burning and she said they were on fire. She walked up to me and said look at my hands they're burning their own fire, we laughed and agreed yes God will use you today and little did we know what was about to transpire. See on this reservation there was a couple, a lady and her husband. The husband had a very serious problem with alcohol and drinking and abusing it every Friday and Saturday. He would abuse it to the point where he would be drunk and go home drunk. Well, his wife had got tired of it and told him "Do not come back to this house drunk ever again". Well, he didn't listen to his wife and went home on this Saturday night drunk as he had always been doing. The man's wife could not take it anymore and had warned him and warned him. When he came to that door drunk, she picked up a hatchet and chopped her husband on the side of his head with it. She then picked up the phone and called 911 and tell them that she had just killed her husband and to come pick him up. The ambulance arrived at the house and the paramedics went in and were in shock. They said that the man was lying in a pool of blood, they said they had never seen that much blood in their life.

They put the man on this stretcher and put him in the ambulance and drove him immediately to the hospital where Sharon was just happened to be working. When they brought the man into the hospital there were three other doctors working over Sharon and they told her to clean the man up and get all the blood and stuff from his body and get him ready so that the Indians can bury him. This was the purpose that God was using her for because she cleaned the blood from the man and went to work on him. She uses numerous towels and bed sheets to try to stop the bleeding. God use her to remove the hatchet from the man's skull and she put a metal plate in his head after putting his brain back in his skull also. Sharon then closed the wound and gave him plenty of blood transfusion. It's funny that I got to witness all of this because I took my wife dinner like I do every night to the hospital. Don't you know the doctors asked Sharon what was the time of death for this man and she said he's still alive and the doctors were in shock. With all the blood that this man had lost they could not believe he was still alive, and that Sharon had done all of this and kept him alive she saved his life.

I will never as long as I live forget what happened that night God used Sharon to the fullest and saved a man's life, until this day he goes to church every Sunday with his wife and do not drink alcohol anymore, so I know we touched lives and saved many people as God would have us to do his will. And now we know why her hands was burning and on fire, that was the spirit of God in her hands leading her and showing her what to do. We continue to reminisce and talk about all this time that we had helped so many people and I thank God for that. then that night Sharon and I, listen to gospel music that we really enjoy. One thing that I always think about is that early in our relationship when we had just met, I remember telling Sharon that I go to my sister Joyce grave every day and she tell me yes, I know Joyce told me. At the time I really didn't think anything of it. So, minute by minute and hour by hour we continue to talk and reminisce and hold each other seems like all through the night. Love is an amazing thing and makes you feel good all over. But ask those up in high places and they don't have a clue what I'm speaking about. It's all about their little money, or degrees or their children or something other than the creator that they have their heart and mind into.

That night before Sharon's surgery I told her I said you remind me of Joyce. Your life has touched and impacted thousands and thousands of people across the world. I'll tell her I remember in Danville VA one day I went up to the mall to get me a new pair of jeans. While walking through the mall I ran into our home economics teacher. This lady was one of the best teachers Joyce and I ever had in school. A very nice lady Joyce had become one of her favorite students that she just loves so much. Joyce really made a big impact on this teacher's life, and I remember the teacher saying that Joyce was one of her favorite students.

The teacher saw me in the mall and came up to me so happy and cheerful and asking me how I was doing, and how is life going since high school. And I really enjoyed talking to her until she asked me how Joyce doing, where is Joyce. I told the teacher that Joyce was no longer here. And this teacher said oh she moved out of town tell her I said hello. Again, I had to reply and said no she's not here I had to make it plain to the teacher that Joyce had been killed. When I said this, this

30

teacher started shaking and crying and screaming right there in the mall in front of me and she had her family with her. Everyone was looking it was something I will never forget and then I slowly walked off, but I could still hear her as I walked away slowly her screaming see this is love Joyce had made a big impact on this teacher's life as the teacher has made a tremendous impact in our lives.

Well, the day of the surgery has come, and we get up feeling very nervous, me and Sharon. I remember we got up and the children and I and Sharon, we get together in the living room with the two grandbabies at this time. We formed a circle and joined hands and one of the children prayed. After we prayed, I looked at Sharon, I looked at her feet as she walked across that living room floor, Just like Sharon had taken care of me with my battle with sarcoidosis, I was more than prepared to take care of my beautiful, lovely wife with her battle with Chiari malformation. At the end of the day a child of God will always do battle, we are on the battlefield for our God.

I drove her to the hospital with the children and grandbabies and they prepared my wife for surgery and then the surgery started. It was supposed to be a three-to-four-hour surgery, but it lasted over 6 hours before it was over, and they kept me updated and posted on everything that was going on.

The nurse came and got me and took me to the recovery room where Sharon was resting. I was so glad to see my wife, but I could tell she was in tremendous pain, and at one point she stated that she was in tremendous pain. We talked but I didn't want to talk too much because I wanted her to rest. There was a cup of ice sitting on the tray that was beside her and I asked did she want some chips of ice and she said, "yes please". Sharon didn't say too much because of the pain she was in, but I can see a lot in her eyes because she was my soul mate, I could read her eyes and what they were saying. I stayed in the room with her until she was able to go home so there was an extra bed in the room for me. I was very tired so I was walking over to this bed to lay down and as 1 [1] m walking over, I say to Sharon "I love you and I will never leave you ever", Sharon replied "I know, and I love you too and thank you for giving me the best life". Don't you know something told me to turn around and when I did, she was gone! Sharon was not breathing or moving, and I immediately called for help, and the nurse's station was right in front of her room so they could see everything.

I will never forget this day because I must remember this day and relive this day for the rest of my life. I have lost the love of my life and best friend. I could not breathe, I started to panic I have become so sick while they were trying to work on Sharon and bring her back, I became very ill. My wife was gone. I yelled and scream, I just did not want to live anymore. The best and most important part of me was gone.

I'm a minister and a child of God, I was so angry that all I could do is ask GOD why, why God! The Lord God had to sit me down and explain to me that we are on the battlefield doing battle and we will get wounded and killed on the battlefield. I Understood what my savor was saying, but I was so very hurt. Now I had to lay my wife to rest, and Sharon being an organ donor, they used a great deal of Sharon's organs and tissue and blood to help save a lot of people lives out in Arizona, and I've received many letters from people she helped save, while in her death she's saving people.

Don't you know that all the scripture of the Bible has been fulfilled in Sharon and me, because of our pure unwavering love for God and making him first and only and true love. The Bible plainly tells anybody in first John 4th chapter 7th and 8th verse it reads beloved, let us love one another, for love is from God and whoever loves has been born of God and knows God. anyone who does not love does not know God, because God is love.

So, after talking with my family and still having to battle my sickness, I decided to move back to Virginia and have my wife buried there as well. The hardest thing to do in my life was to bury my wife. To bury the best, and I mean the very best part of me. I contacted the Funeral Home and set up the service with my family's help. I gave my wife her military homegoing, only fitting for a military soldier. The Funeral Home had requested me to give them a dress to bury my wife in, don't you know my mother had a purple suit that she gave me to bury my wife in, and being her favorite color, she loved purple. The whole entire time doing the funeral I couldn't do anything, but cry. Doing the funeral reception, the undertaker at the funeral home, introduced himself to me and said, "I have been married to my wife over 30 years" he said, "I don't know what I would do if I lost my wife". He said also "I'm sorry for your loss" and gave me a hug. That has stayed with me and show me that he was a good man and cared earnestly about what was going on with me. Well, we had my wife homegoing and now I have become a widower, at the graveside the military presented me with the American flag for her service in the Navy. Stress is a huge factor in sarcoidosis progression and worrisome. I was in a great deal of pain as you can imagine during this time, I called our doctor who is back in phoenix AZ and asked if he could write me a prescription for some pain medicine and he said that he couldn't because I was not there in Arizona, I was in so much pain. My life had flashed before my eyes and I had concluded that I had to start all over, I was like a child that was lost so I kept right on praying and reading my father's holy words. Don't you know that after we had my wife's funeral the children and I had to drive back over 2700 miles to get back home. With God's help we did, but in Dallas TX we came across a very bad Blizzard and the roads were very hard to travel with the snow and ice. Memories of how we treated someone are the only thing we can take out of this life. Oh yes you will remember forever how you treated someone good or bad it will haunt you forever and now that I think about it most people are being haunted by how they treated people when they were alive. I would have to walk the rest of my life through this valley and shadow of death life all by myself now. When we got back home to Arizona, I thought about what I had to do and that would be to let everyone know that my wife is no longer here, just like I did with my sister Joyce. I thank God with all my heart for everyone HE has placed in my wife and I life.

Sharon death was a shock to the world at 44 years old. She made such an impact on her job that the Native Americans asked me can they have their own funeral for her. This made me very happy that they thought so much of my wife and of course I said yes. They asked if I would write something to be read at the ceremony for her and it was my pleasure to do so. The letter that I wrote was so touching everyone present shed had tears for her. Sharon was the first and only American to have a native homegoing celebration on this reservation. I am so proud of my wife, again we had true unconditional love.

After the ceremony everyone hugged and gave me cards of condolence. Sharon brought so much happiness and joy to every reservation we ever lived on. One of her favorite things was the "pow wow" festivals. We even participated in the ceremonies, which were totally amazing. She would volunteer me for everything as well as herself. When I got back home, I went to her Facebook page which was her favorite thing to do was to look at Facebook. Until this day the post is still there that I said about my wife. I posted on her page and it's there for everyone to see. Well, I started calling around every job she ever worked in and was telling them that Sharon had passed away and I got a lot of people very upset and angry and in disbelief. Nobody could believe that Sharon was gone.

I went by her favorite restaurant to get breakfast, and when I pulled up the girl that had been serving Sharon for years came to the window of the drive through and smiled. See Sharon had eaten breakfast here every day, until the girl just knew what she wanted and had it ready. The girl handed me the bag and said where is your wife, I just held my head down and when I looked up at the girl, she knew something was not right. I looked this girl in the eyes, and I said she's gone. The girl looked puzzled and said when will she be back, I said she passed away and this girl's face became as if she's seen a ghost. She began to cry and shed tears. As I began to cry, we shed tears together and I slowly drove away. That very next day I went to check on our friend, and the manager said that she had quit. Maybe she felt that her purpose at the restaurant had been served. Yes, the love that Sharon and I share in this life, the world will never know the true meaning of love. The life that we live doing this small lifetime this world will never know what it's like to try and live for the creator of this universe. This world will never know what two flesh and two spirits joined together to make one is like. The meaning of human creation is to serve one another, and the world will never know the true meaning. It baffles me because everyone claimed to love Jesus, and this is all he ever did was serve. But again, God say that people serve HIM with their mouth and their hearts are far from HIM. But as for me and my house, we will serve the Lord forever and ever. When this life is over all the Saints will sit at HIS feet and be blessed. Like I said before memories are all we have to take out of this world, and I know my wife had nothing but great memories of me, she told me every day. I think all the time about the memories and adventures that we had. I will always treasure my wife legacy of doing for others. I continue every day to fight and do battle with this disease, sarcoidosis. It has started becoming more and more of a problem. I had one doctor to start helping me in Virginia and this doctor told me that he knew all about sarcoidosis and that he would treat me until I passed away, being that there is no cure for the disease. Don't you know, three weeks after my first visit, this doctor himself passed away and it shocked me. I went to the hospital because I was having chest pains and I found out that I had a blockage of my heart.

I became so sick I applied for disability and was denied yet again, but I let nothing stop me from doing my father's will. I remember laying in the bed crying in so much pain and out the corner of my eye was an Angel there at my feet. This Angel spoke to me and said get up we have work to do, and don't you know four weeks after that I was driving tractor trailer. To drive tractor trailers you must take and pass a Department of Transportation physical and yes, I barely passed, and I did not mention all my sicknesses during the physical. Getting my CDL was a great and ultimate task for me, and I had no idea of the adventures that awaited me. You can do more in the spirit than you ever could in the flesh. I was working for a good trucking company but on the road in the truck it gets very lonely. So, after being alone for a long time, I thought that I would join one of the dating websites. I've found out that men don't have much to choose from out there in the world and women don't have much to choose from neither, so it goes both ways. I talked to many women on the dating website, and it appears to me that they all had a motive and I'm sure they say the same about men. I was not looking for someone to replace my wife, there was only one Sharon. I was just looking to see if love did exist again. One lady I met in particular her name is "Vee". I got to know "Vee" and she got to know me. We talked over the phone for a while and then we agreed to meet. When we met, we started to date eventually, and I've got to meet her children she had three girls, adult girls. "Vee" is special, and she did know what Love Is all about, she herself was married and lost her husband due to sickness. She met my family and gave me one of the best Thanksgiving dinners since the loss of my wife Sharon. I will always remember that Thanksgiving dinner she fixed for me, and my family even though certain people didn't like it, she cooked dinner there at my mother's house. "Vee" is one of the hardest working, beautiful ladies I know. "Vee" is an only child and very spoiled and that's not bad. I was truly blessed by God that he led me to find "Vee". Don't you know that "Vee" left her apartment and quit three jobs that she was working to travel and be with me and we lived very comfortably in the tractor trailer truck. By the way, "Vee" lived in Atlanta, Georgia and I was living in Danville, Virginia. I told "Vee" about my battle with sarcoidosis, and she would do research on it and found that another celebrity had it also. I try my best to make "Vee" happy and we would go to the movies and out to eat and do things for each other. One thing "Vee" done for me was we got dressed up and she took me to a restaurant and the plate was over $100 per person. The food was superb. She done this for me on my birthday and it brought back memories of how Sharon would Take Me Out to eat on my birthday as well. And of course, when "Vee" had her birthday, I would do things for her and let her go shopping. "Vee" and I traveled all over the United States and had a great time. We went to places like New York, Chicago, Indiana, Florida, Kentucky, Tennessee, New Jersey, Texas, North Carolina, South Carolina, and many other places. I would also call her mother and talk with her, and she would call me from time to time. I remember one day her mother asked me, "do you love my daughter" and I said, "yes ma'am I do". Her mother was so overjoyed to hear these words come out of my mouth that I loved her daughter, and I truly did, and she witnessed it by me taking care of her daughter on the road.

"Vee" had the chance to go places and see things that her mother couldn't because of her obligations to raising her. And this made her mother so very happy to know that her daughter was going places and doing things that she didn't have the opportunity to ever do. "Vee" told me that the most beautiful thing was the snow in Chicago. Being from Florida born and raised and moving to Georgia, they did not see much snow and now she got to not only see snow but be in the middle of a Blizzard in Chicago and she really enjoyed the snow. There was nothing that "Vee" would not do for me, and there is nothing that I would not do for "Vee".

"VEE" mother became sick while on the road, so "vee" had to get off the road and go home to be with her sweet mother.

In turn of events her beautiful, loving mother whom I also love, passed away and this hurt "vee" so much and me as well. I will always regret not being there for "vee" and her mother in time of need. I was on the road when her mother passed. I was in Chicago, and it was a very bad blizzard. I couldn't get out of Chicago and if I could it was way too dangerous for me to travel.

This changed our relationship, but we were always close friends. So, I was driving and working, but alone again. As a truck driver traveling great distances all you have is time. Time to think about your life and things that you should have done that you didn't do. I remember talking to my mother while on the road and she said, "you eating some good food out there on the road"? I would tell her yes, because I did eat very good out on the road in different states. So, I just drive all over the United States and witness to as many that I come across, about the goodness of GOD. I met some interesting people while on the road. One nice lady I had the pleaser to get to know was Tonya. She lived close to Danville. We talked about GOD every day. She had been battling cancer and GOD saved her twice. While sitting in the living room, I remember seeing the sparkles in her eyes as I talk with the love and grace of GOD. One day Tonya told me that she had a young family member who was a you lady and had just got married. DON'T YOU KNOW that this young lady had been hemorrhaging for 16 years and the doctors did not know why. She was also depressed because she wanted a child and couldn't have one. Well Tonya had been listening to me talk about how GOD has and still to this very day, use me to help people. Tonya asked me do I have any Anointing oil. I said yes, I do and gave her some oil to give to this young lady. She took the oil and ANOINTED herself and her home and don't you know she stopped bleeding and had a child. This is why I don't care to play with GOD, or to have a form of GODLYNESS. Tonya fixed me dinner every day after work, and she fixed me lunch to take to work every day. She was sick on top of everything, but she didn't let it get her down. I remember she asked me if I could be her caregiver, but she knew I was under a contract with my job. But I would have done it in a heartbeat. I love people, Tonya had a beautiful grandson and he loved me I know, and I loved him also. Well one day I took Tonya and her grandson fishing. Tonya had never in her life been fishing and it was a joy to see her smiling and happy. I even stopped at a store to get another fishing pole and got her grandson a toy that cost $48 dollars. We had a wonderful day. Tonya passed away on the battlefield for our LORD. See I do not posses no heaven or HELL to send nobody to and like 2 Corinthians the 5th chapter and the 8th verse say "we are confident, I say, and willing rather to be absent from the body and to be present with the LORD.

Truck driving is not a job, but a way of life. I have had a lot of close calls with death as all truck drivers have, I have seen more deaths on the highway than I care to think about. You have got to be careful on the roads. There is a GOD and HE will take care of you. Wintertime is a very bad time for truck driving. I was coming out of CHICAGO one day and it was sleeting. Sleet is those pellets of ice precipitation that fall, and this is the worst thing for a truck driver to drive in. Well, while going down the road from Chicago the traffic was very heavy. A female police officer had come to a complete stop and had exit her police cruiser, to check on a woman that had skid off the road.

Thank GOD I was only going 35 miles per hour, but even at that speed I lost control of the truck and all 18 tires, I locked them up and prayed. Don't you know I slid right up to the bumper of that police car while the officer was passing by, and she was so focused on the car that had skid off the road that she didn't really see me almost hit her. That truck stopped just inches from hitting her. It's very dangerous out there. I remember going to SEAITLE, WASHINGTON from OAKLAHOMA CITY, OAKLAHOMA. I had a very nice trip till I got to IDAHO. I ran into a blizzard in IDAHO. While driving down this mountain there were a lot of big trucks and a road plow in front of me plowing the road and putting down salt. I had my CB on and was listening. Don't you know that snowplow slid off the road in front of me and it was a lady driving. As I checked in my mirrors, I could see trucks sliding off the road one by one. | was praying very hard at this point, and not one time did I slide, not to mention that we were supposed to have chain up anyway. At my age I had not seen this much snow in my entire life, I know it was GOD that brought me safe down that mountain, because I was the only truck that made it down and I counted 6 trucks behind me and there was 4 trucks and a road plow in front of me. Thank GOD everybody was fine, And as you can imagen this happened to me more than once. OHIO can get a lot of snow also. I recall one early morning the day before Christmas, I was trying to get home to Danville, VIRGINIA. I had just filled my truck up, and I noticed a state trooper walking over to me. He asked if I was going to get on the road, and I said yes, I am. The road conditions were critical for driving. The roads had not been cleaned and it was like driving at your own risk. So, this nice tall gentleman explains to me that he was trying to go 4 miles down the road to get home to be with his wife and daughter for Christmas. It was so much snow that it came up to the bumper of his police cruiser. He kindly asked me if I could lay down some tracks for him and I replied, I sure can. I was more than happy to help him get home. See, the road was so covered with snow that you could only see a faint outline of where a road could be. GOD is so good, I prayed, because I couldn't see no road, but i knew this road very well, I had taken it hundreds of times. I slowly pulled onto the highway and proceeded to lay the tracks down using this big truck. The speed limit is 70 on this highway, but we could only do 25 mph safely.

I was using the front of the truck to push snow out our way and to make tracks. I constantly checked my mirrors to make sure the officer was ok. DON'T YOU KNOW that after 4 miles he turned on his siren and lights and was just waving to thank me for doing it. I felt very good helping him, but I had yet over 200 miles to get home myself in all this snow. So, I continued to drive on, and being the only vehicle on the road I didn't have to worry about too much, but just focus on trying not to slide off the highway. What it was, a Blizzard had come through this part of OHIO and many people may remember, it was very bad.

Something said to me, "keep driving, you will soon run out of all the snow." I was obedient and drove about 20 miles at 25 and 30 mph and DON'T YOU KNOW the sky started to clear up and I began to see a better outline of the road. The more I pressed down the road the better the road conditions became and by the time I got to WEST VIRGINIA, the highway was better to travel, and I made it home to VIRGINIA safe with no incident.

In my tucking career I have now been to every state, and I remember when I had to spend the night in the Bronx, NEW YORK. No matter where I go and no matter what I do, my mind always goes back to my wife and best friend. I love to eat, so I remember on my birthday one year, my sweet wife took me out to eat at a nice restaurant. I had a very lovely time, and our waitress was very nice. My wife and I had a connection to the point we didn't have to say anything, because we knew what each other was thinking. So, after we finished eating, we smiled at each other, because we knew what was coming next, We both new that I had $500 dollars in my wallet and that we were going to be a blessing to this young lady by the power of our GOD. I remember very clearly that when she came with the bill, Sharon and I just all smiling. Sharon paid for my birthday dinner, and I went into my wallet and took out the $500 dollars and placed it in the young lady's hand. She looked at me puzzled and said, "oh she already paid." I said, "no that's for you waiting on us." This young lady started to scream out loud and cry right there in the restaurant in front of everybody. The manager ran over to see what was going on. When he seen the money in her hand and I told him a gave her a tip, then he started to cry. See, our waitress was pregnant and working very hard to prepare a life for her baby that was due in a few weeks the manager told us. He told us that the boyfriend left her and that she didn't have anything for the baby. She was a very nice young, white lady, And the thing about me and my wife, we don't care who you are, we stive to help everybody. On my birthday, that made my day. Ironically DON'T YOU KNOW the same thing similar to this happened the same year on Sharon's Birthday, just 5 months after mine. Only difference is Sharon liked Chinese food so that's where we ate at on her birthday, and the waitress had just lost her mother and was having hard time to pay for burial expenses, that's what she told us after I tipped her $300. She was so happy, to the point of thanking us all the way to the door. I never will forget when Sharon told me, she said, "You will give the shirt off your back to anybody," and I looked into her beautiful brown eyes and said, "Yes I will, if they need it."

That's what I do while focusing on the traffic and the day that's before me, I just think about all the good days my wife and I had. At the end of the day when we leave this old world all we can take out from this world are the memories of how evil and mean we were to people. That's what most people might remember, but I have more good memories of myself than bad memories. Time on this earth is short and people will support this and support that and I know that supporting what's right is not a popular thing to do. This is a backwards world. Like I said before I have witnessed more death on the highway than I care to think about. Please be safe out their fellow truck drivers, because just like in ministry, we as pastors of GOD are held to a higher standard, because GOD expect more from us. In trucking we are held to a higher standard as a professional driver. We must go from point (A) to point (B) in a safe manner and keep the public safe in doing so. I have driven millions of miles with no tickets and no accident, and if anybody knew the places I have been, you will know that there's a GOD somewhere. I mean I have gotten plenty of inspection tickets and passed every one of them for having everything in order and up to date. There are families and little children and babies traveling on these roads in vehicles and we must keep them safe by any and all means necessary. Our biggest job is to keep the public safe while we service the public. People from all walks of life are truck drivers. I met a model from NEW YORK CITY who appeared on the cover of vogue magazine. She bought her a truck and said she likes to travel, that's why she is driving big riggs. I met a doctor who had moved his family to America from China. He became a truck driver and took a break from surgery he said. And they have a 13-year-old son, and the mother home-schooled him right there in the truck. They love it, he told me. I have seen and met some famous movie stars too, as they travel from place to place. One thing that bothers me as a human being and as a truck driver. I love and have helped people from all corners of this world and I'm not a racist. The little children LOVE the big trucks, and they wave at us all the time and motion for us to blow that big air horn. That fascinates them. Well, one Saturday, I passed through downtown Milwaukee, Wisconsin and was heading down south and I found a truck stop to take a break and get me something to eat. I took my exit and was going to turn left and head to the truck stop.

I came up to the light and this light lasted for a long time. I had never seen a light last so long. Soon enough a white Toyota Camry pulled up beside me. Sitting up high in a truck, we can see all in the car. I had seen in this car two ladies in the front. One was older and one was younger, but in the back seat there was a young child in the back seat. This little child took her seatbelt off and turned her back to the ladies in the front and she looked at me and waved and got back in her seat and put her seatbelt back on. The light still hadn't turned green, and the ladies were just talking as I could see, and they were deep in their conversation so much that they didn't even notice the little girl got out of her seat. Being from the south, from Danville Virginia, I knew what this was about. I knew that she wanted to wave like all children and even adults do, but I feared for her life. There is no telling what those women would have done to the little girl for waving at a black man. Children are taught hate from an early age, and they were teaching this child to hate, but the little girl wasn't learning hate. And they all had on white dresses like they had been to church. GOD allowed me to witness that and so much more while on the road. And speaking of church, I came up to a church and was driving slow on the tractor trailer to be safe and to show respect. The service had ended, and they were coming out. While at a red light right at that church a car pulled up and I look down and there was this old white gentleman driving and this old white lady sticking her middle finger up at me and sticking her tongue out at me. This really put me in a bad mood that day. So, running to church doesn't mean anything is what I thought to myself. We as truck drivers like it when the public wave at us to show us that you are proud of us risking our life and being away from our family to service yours.

I became very ill from this sarcoidosis one day and had to come off the road and go to the doctor. I went to the doctor in so much pain I couldn't stand it. I was in unbearable pain.

The doctor called me in the room and see that I'm a truck driver from my file. He started to shake my hand. DON'T YOU KNOW this man just kept saying thank you for doing a good job and looked me right in the eye and said that my job is more important than his job. I couldn't believe this. He was pointing at all the equipment in the office and said I can't do my job without truck drivers. I had been told this by a lot of doctors and to this day, I'm still being told the same thing. And guess what, it feels good to know that the public acknowledge the importance of our job. So as a pastor and a truck driver I am doing two of the most important jobs in the world. Leading the lost to JESUS and suppling the stores with food and moving the mail and packages and I have done it all. I love it when we as truck drivers make people happy. I recall being down in South Carolina and this black SUV pulled up along side of me with dark tented windows. I looked and all the windows started to go down. There was a lady and she had 4 little children in the car, and I heard her say look at the big truck. The children were just waving and jumping up and down, they were so happy to see the big truck.

This happens to me all the time. The adults are equally exited as well to see the big rigs. Nobody knows what we are going through. One day I had a delivery to pick up in a small town one hundred miles above NEW YORK CITY. This town had restricted roads for big trucks. It's a very small town. Well, I drove into this town and was following my GPS. The time was one o'clock in the morning and I'm in this town trying to find this customer. The GPS is telling me to make a right turn and I did, but I should have paid more close attention. I stared to go down this road and quickly found out that no truck has ever been down this road. The pavement turned into gravel and then as I continued the gravel turned into dirt and I knew I was in trouble with no way possible to turn around or to try and back out, there was just no way. began to pray very hard because I knew that a Crain would have to come and lift that truck and trailer out of there. I continued to drive on this dirt road at a snail pace. I couldn't go no more than five MPH. I was pushing down trees and everything. This definitely was a restricted road for trucks. I just kept right on praying and through the trees and bushes I could see a store. I said to myself, if I could just make it to that store. Eventually I made it to that store and pulled up and put my head down on the steering wheel. In just a few minutes a red mustang pulls up right beside me. The man driving said to me, "Driver how are you going to get THAT out of here." I looked at him and said, "Sir I don't know." The nice gentleman said, "I am a retired truck driver, I will lead you back to the highway." He said, "you going to push down some trees, but don't hit any of the cars." I was so thankful GOD had sent me help just like that and there were cars parked all along the road and I didn't hit anything. I went to the rest area not far away and went to sleep and DON'T YOU KNOW the next morning I found the place. In the daylight I seen where I made a right turn and should have made a left turn. We as truck drivers make mistakes, but we can't harm the public no matter what..

I would just like to take out a few moments to honor my beautiful and magnificent wife in my autobiography with some of her achievements and accomplishments that meant a lot to her. With five wonderful children Sharon, being the woman and daughter of GOD ALMIGHTY, knew what she had to do, and like a strong woman she surpassed and excelled. Not most people believe to much of anything anymore, but don't you know that LOVE and RESPECT will take you where you need to be in life.

My wife even holds a letter from the president of the UNITED STATES, PRESIDENT MR. BILL CLINTON, the 42 nd president and he congratulates my wife SHARON for all the many accomplishments and her service to this country in the U.S. NAVY. FROM THE BOTTOM OF MY HEART, MRS. SHARON KAYE FITZGERALD, I JUST SAY THANK YOU!!! (WE MADE IT MY LOVE)

This is one of my favorite pictures. Sharon said, "don't take that picture," to the photographer. She moved over close as we could get and that's what she wanted, then he took our picture. I PRAISE GOD for MEMORY!

Department of the Navy

This is to certify that

SHARON KAYE JONES

has

COMPLETED THE COURSE FOR RECRUIT RELIGIOUS COORDINATOR

given at

THE RECRUIT CHAPEL

RECRUIT TRAINING COMMAND

ORLANDO, FLORIDA

07 MAY _____ 19 89

_____
DIRECTOR, RTC CHAPEL

DEGREES

CONTINUED FROM PAGE 1B

...owed up to wave signs that said "Congratulations Renea" and "We love you Renea."

Wells James, too, began her academic journey at an untraditional age. She's 38 and graduated cum laude with a bachelor's degree in sociology.

"We are very proud of her," said her sister, Diana Wells of Atlanta. "We are super elated to see her reach this milestone."

Wake County Schools Superintendent Bill McNeal, recently named the nation's top superintendent by the American Association of School Administrators, delivered the commencement address. McNeal received his bachelor's and master's degrees from NCCU in 1971 and 1976, respectively, and has spent more than 25 years in the Wake

Sharon Wright smiles before receiving her bachelor's degree in nursing. 'I didn't dream that I would be here,' she says.

schools.

He also met his wife, Faye, at NCCU and started to talk Saturday about a particular rendezvous near the stadium during their college days. But then he stopped. "You're not cleared for that information," he told the grads.

The laughter signaled that they had drawn a particularly racy conclusion, which meant they took the bait.

"Actually, it was a proposal," McNeal said. "I know where your heads are, even at 8:30 in the morning."

McNeal drew upon the movie classic "The Wizard of Oz" and the landmark U.S. Supreme Court desegregation decision Brown v. Board of Education to show the graduates how family, friends and professors had led them to this day by helping them realize their potential.

"A message for every last one of our graduates should be that they have the brains, the heart, the courage and home, not only to succeed, but to lead," McNeal said.

Staff writer Dan Kane
can be reached at 829-4861
or dkane@newsobserver.com.

DEGREES

CONTINUED FROM PAGE 1B

owed up to wave signs that said 'ongratulations Renea" and "We ve you Renea."

Wells James, too, began her academic journey at an untraditional e. She's 38 and graduated cum ide with a bachelor's degree in ciology.

"We are very proud of her," said r sister, Diana Wells of Atlanta. Ve are super elated to see her ach this milestone."

Wake County Schools Superintendent Bill McNeal, recently med the nation's top superinadent by the American Association of School Administrators, livered the commencement adess. McNeal received his bachr's and master's degrees from CCU in 1971 and 1976, reectively, and has spent more an 25 years in the Wake

Sharon Wright smiles before receiving her bachelor's degree in nursing. 'I didn't dream that I would be here,' she says.

schools.

He also met his wife, Faye, at NCCU and started to talk Saturday about a particular rendezvous near the stadium during their college days. But then he stopped. "You're not cleared for that information," he told the grads.

The laughter signaled that they had drawn a particularly racy conclusion, which meant they took the bait.

"Actually, it was a proposal," McNeal said. "I know where your heads are, even at 8:30 in the morning."

McNeal drew upon the movie classic "The Wizard of Oz" and the landmark U.S. Supreme Court desegregation decision Brown v. Board of Education to show the graduates how family, friends and professors had led them to this day by helping them realize their potential.

"A message for every last one of our graduates should be that they have the brains, the heart, the courage and home, not only to succeed, but to lead," McNeal said.

Staff writer Dan Kane can be reached at 829-4861 or dkane@newsobserver.com.

Mother of 5 and PCC stu
leads both college, state

Sharon Wright-Watson is a Navy veteran, an associate pastor and studying to be a nurse

By BONNIE DAVIS
Director of Public Information
Piedmont Community College

Piedmont Community College student Sharon Wright-Watson didn't anticipate the whirlwind of events that has thrust her into a visible statewide position, but this remarkable mother of five is a dynamo of energy who welcomes the opportunity to make a difference.

Wright-Watson has been named president of the N4CSGA, the state Student Government Association for North Carolina's 59 schools in the state Community College System. In that capacity, she sits as an ex officio member of the State Board of Community Colleges, the policy-making arm for the system. She came to the state leadership position by virtue of her election as president of PCC's SGA, which also gives her ex officio membership on PCC's board of trustees for the current year.

Not too long ago, Wright-Watson had agreed to serve as N4CSGA vice president, a job she thought she could handle while keeping up with her family and studies. But when the N4CSGA president had to step down, she was asked to step up, and she agreed.

Within a week's time, she found herself answering a reporter's questions following a state board meeting in Raleigh.

She is one of three Person County-area persons serving in state community college leadership positions this year. Roxboro resident James Woody was recently installed as the State Board of Community Colleges chairman, and PCC President Dr. H. James Owen was elected president of the N.C. Association of Community College

Ken Martin / C-T

SHARON WRIGHT-WATSON: 'I just want to help people.'

recent state and PCC board meetings. Her background in the military and as a parent as well as a student give her a broad base of experience from which to draw.

A resident of Milton, she was graduated from Bartlett Yancey High School in 1987. At BYHS, she had earned her credentials as a certified nursing assistant, and she went to work as a CNA at two Danville, Va. health care facilities. She entered the U.S. Navy in 1989 and worked in aviation ordnance building bombs and loading them

tary since she joined the Army National Guard in June 2000.

After studying cosmetology at PCC earlier in her life, Wright-Watson became reacquainted with PCC in March 1999 when, as a divorced mother of five children, she needed assistance. She entered PCC's Work First program and met PCC counselor Brian Totten, who encouraged her and learned she still wanted to pursue her earlier interest in nursing. He suggested she come to PCC and talk to an academic

𝔘nited 𝔖tates 𝔖enate

WASHINGTON, DC 20510–3301

March 29, 2002

Ms. Sharon Wright-Watson
11376 NC Hwy 62N
Milton, North Carolina 27305

Dear Ms. Wright-Watson:

Thank you for your recent letter in support of the TRIO program. Needless to say, I have heard from many school officials–and students–on this one.

Rest assured, there are currently no proposals in Congress to eliminate or drastically decrease the funding for the TRIO program. I will keep your concerns in mind when funding for the TRIO program is being considered in the Senate.

I appreciate your letting me hear from you.

Kindest regards.

Sincerely,

Jesse Helms

JESSE HELMS:rm

In Appreciation

Presented To

Sharon Wright-Watson
2001 - 2002 President

For dedicated service to the N4CSGA.

Uma Bond
_____
Advisor

_____
Advisor

_____
Advisor

_____
Trustee

47

In Appreciation

Presented To

Sharon Wright-Watson

2001 - 2002 President

For dedicated service to the NACSGA.

_____
Advisor

_____
Advisor

_____
Advisor

_____
Trustee

State of North Carolina
Office of the Lieutenant Governor

BEVERLY EAVES PERDUE
LIEUTENANT GOVERNOR

310 NORTH BLOUNT STREET
20401 MAIL SERVICE CENTER
RALEIGH, NC 27699-0401

TELEPHONE: (919) 733-7350
FAX: (919) 733-6595
e-mail: bperdue@ncmail.net

April 27, 2004

Ensign Sharon K. Wright-Watson
1570 Town House #B
Crooked Branch Road
Creedmoor, NC 27522

Dear Sharon:

Thank you for your kind letter, it really touched my heart and I am very proud of your efforts to make a better life for you and your children. I am sorry that my schedule prevents me from being able to attend your commencement exercise and pinning ceremony. Please know, however, that your accomplishments are inspirational not just to single parents, but to anyone working towards their goals and dreams.

You are so right, Sharon, in saying that "education is the key." It will open many doors for you and your children. It is your determination, however, that made it possible for you to finish your education while raising 5 wonderful children and keeping hope and faith in your life and theirs. I am honored that you consider me an inspiration in your life – but I must say, your story has been an inspiration to my own.

Sincerely,

Beverly E. Perdue

BEP:aj

STATE OF NORTH CAROLINA
OFFICE OF THE GOVERNOR
20301 MAIL SERVICE CENTER • RALEIGH, NC 27699-0301

MICHAEL F. EASLEY
GOVERNOR

April 28, 2004

Ms. Sharon K. Wright
1570 Town House #B
Crooked Branch Road
Creedmoor, NC 27522

Dear Ms. Wright:

Congratulations on your upcoming graduation from North Carolina Central University with a degree in nursing. I appreciate the kind invitation to join the celebration on May 1, 2004, and regret that my schedule does not permit me to do so.

When you receive your degree, you will close a chapter of your life that required incredible perseverance and determination, with an unwavering commitment to excellence. I am pleased that the JR/SRCOSTEP Program allowed you to complete your studies while providing a good life for your family. You do indeed serve as an inspiration to others.

The First Lady joins me in extending warm congratulations. As you embark on the next leg of your life's journey, we wish you continued success. Based on your history to make life better for you and your children, we are certain your career will be extraordinary.

With kindest regards, I remain

Very truly yours,

Michael F. Easley

MFE:pbt

May 1, 2004

Ms. Sharon Wright
1570 Apartment B
Crooked Branch Road
Creedmoor, NC 27522

Dear Sharon:

Many heartfelt congratulations on your graduation from North Carolina Central University. Given the path you have taken thus far, I have every confidence that you will find continued success and joy in life.

I know how important education has been to you personally, through your academic and leadership achievements at Piedmont Community College and in student government, your work at Duke University Hospital, and your involvement with higher education issues in our state.

The concerns expressed by you and by other education leaders during the budget process have helped us keep harmful budget cuts away from our public schools, community colleges and universities – and protect the investments we have made in our educational system.

Sharon, you are the type of student – and now, graduate – who shows us just how important those investments are. Today you can celebrate the fact that all your hard work has paid off. I know you will use your success to continue to make life better for those around you, and to continue to give back to your community and your state. I am so very proud of you, and I hope you will enjoy and remember this day for the rest of your life. Again, best wishes for continued success, and congratulations.

Sincerely,

Marc Basnight

North Carolina Central University

DURHAM, NORTH CAROLINA
A MEMBER OF THE UNIVERSITY OF NORTH CAROLINA SYSTEM

TO ALL TO WHOM THESE PRESENTS MAY COME, GREETINGS

The Board of Trustees of the University upon recommendation of the Faculty

has conferred upon

Sharon K. Wright-Watson

the degree of

Bachelor of Science in Nursing

with all the rights, honors and privileges thereto appertaining

In Testimony Whereof, we have hereunto subscribed our names and caused the Seal of the University to be affixed at Durham, North Carolina, this the first day of May, 2004.

CHAIRMAN OF THE BOARD OF GOVERNORS
OF THE UNIVERSITY OF NORTH CAROLINA

PRESIDENT OF THE UNIVERSITY
OF NORTH CAROLINA

CHANCELLOR

CHAIRMAN OF THE BOARD OF TRUSTEES

United States Department of Justice

Federal Bureau of Prisons

Federal Law Enforcement Training Center

Glynco, Georgia

Certificate of Graduation

This is to certify that

Sharon Wright

has successfully completed all requirements and has attained the proficiency necessary for graduation from Introduction to Correctional Techniques

Director, Staff Training Academy

September 17, 2004

The Annual
NATIONAL
DAY OF
PRAYER
First Thursday of May

December 21, 2004

Minister Sharon Wright
17 Nellis Terrace
Hanscom AFB, Mass 01731

Dear Minister Wright:

On behalf of the 2005 Caswell County Prayer Breakfast Committee, I would like to invite you to be a participant in the 3rd annual prayer breakfast held at Carolina Pinnacle Studios. The program starts at 7:00 a.m. and ends by 9:00 a.m. Our theme this year is: "GOD SHED HIS GRACE ON THEE." (Hebrews 4:16 is the supporting verse) We would love to have you with us to share your testimony and whatever God lays upon your heart, including information concerning your book.

It was wonderful to be able to pray with you via telephone on December 8th. What a precious time we shared. I look forward to hearing from you and confirming your participation. May God bless you and your family and may you have a joyful holiday season.

IN HIS SERVICE,

Dale Blackwell-Coons, Chairperson
Caswell County Prayer Breakfast Committee

Attachments

North Carolina Board of Nursing

This is to certify that

SHARON JONES WRIGHT

has this day been registered according to the laws relating to nursing in the State of North Carolina and is entitled to practice as and to hold and use the title of

Registered Nurse

In Witness Whereof, we the undersigned have hereunto set our hand and caused the seal of this Board to be affixed this the 24th of May, 2005.

Certificate No. 201089.

_____
EXECUTIVE DIRECTOR

_____
CHAIR

North Carolina Interventions

This certifies that

Sharon Wright

has fulfilled all requirements for certification and, subject to annual renewal, is qualified to use physical techniques

NCI Interventions - Core + Training

(Parts A and B + designated optional techniques)

A curriculum of the NC Division of Mental Health, Developmental Disabilities andSubstance Abuse Services

Instructor signature

July 18,2005

Date

PCC's Wright-Watson receives State Community College Honor

Piedmont Community College graduate Sharon Wright-Watson of Caswell County was named the recipient of the President's Leadership Award during the State Board of Community College's annual Day of Recognition ceremony on Friday, Nov.15.

Wright-Watson is past president of the NC Community College Comprehensive Student Government Association and past president of the PCC Student Government Association. By virtue of these leadership positions, she also served on the PCC Board of Trustees and the State Board of Community Colleges. Wright-Watson is a 2002 PCC graduate and currently attends NC Central University. She was selected by NCCCS President H. Martin Lancaster to receive the President's Leadership Award.

Wright-Watson has been a vocal advocate for community colleges and community college students, speaking to the State Board, members of the NC General Assembly, and other

WRIGHT–WATSON

agencies as well as the media. She has shared her personal experiences as a former single mother of five children and her attempt to complete her education. A veteran of the U.S. Navy, she currently serves in the Army National Guard. Now remarried, she resides in Milton with her husband, Tommy Lee Watson Jr. and her children. She is active in volunteer work with youth and at her church.

Avalon Administrative Conference

You are hereby credited with 15.7 contact hours for attending this conference, October 11-13, 2006. File #06-09-007.

Presented to:

Sharon Fitzgerald

This educational activity has been approved by the Utah Nurses Association, which is accredited as an approver of continuing education in nursing by the American Nurses Credentialing Center's Commission on Accreditation.

James O. Mason

Avalon President and CEO

Avalon Representative

Conference sponsored by Avalon Management Group

AHCA

Arizona Health Care Care Association

Certificate of Attendance

This is to document that

Sharon Fitzgerald

Attended

"Directors of Nursing Training Course"

October 25-27, 2006 ♦ Plaza Healthcare ♦ Scottsdale, Arizona

Presented by:
Residents First and the Arizona Health Care Association

Signature of Sponsor: _____

Cindy Leach, President, Residents First

Certificate of Achievement

RECOVERY FOUNDATION OF THE SOUTHWEST, INC.

This Certifies That

Sharon Fitzgerald

successfully completed

Creating Harmony in the Workplace
Sponsored by Wassaja Memorial Health Center
In Fort McDowell, Arizona on February 1, 2012

7 contact hours

Richard A. Roddy

Richard A. Roddy, Director

U.S. Department of Health & Human Services

Indian Health Service

Office of
Information Technology

Certificate

Sharon Fitzgerald

has successfully completed

Introduction to the Laboratory
Package

04/05/2012

Joy Holman (Instructor)

Wassaja Memorial Health Center

Certificate of Completion

presents

to

Sharon Fitzgerald, RN

for

Afinion A1C Analyzer Training

Demetra Barr, MD, MPH, FAAFP
FMYN Medical / Health Division Director

June 19, 2012

On behalf of the Health
Department, thank you
for all you do for the
community every day!

— Noam

I completely know and understand that when we depart this life on this planet, we cannot take one thing from off this earth; except for our memories and I thank GOD! See many people won't get or even understand this, but money that the world craves can't make or keep your heart warm inside. The memories that my beautiful wife and I share keep me happy, warm and at peace all day long. All day while driving the Tractor Trailer, I'm focused on the task at hand, but I allow my mind to Rome about all the wonderful times I have had with my wife.

Like this one time I remember I drove to pick Sharon up from work. I open the door for her, and she looks at me and smiles and we smile together. She loves to look at me and I love to look at her and that's the way it has always been. This particular day was different though. While I was driving us home, she looks at me and said, "who is EARL SIMMONS?" I looked at her and said, "that's DARK MAN X." I said to her, "that's DMX the rapper." Sharon had got to meet and take care of the rapper while he was in jail, because she was the nurse at that jail. The level of respect and integrity on my wife's face and the joy in my heart is priceless. Every day that I drive my wife to work we hug, and I say, "Do a good job." She looks at me and smiles with that beautiful smile. I was so proud of my wife for taking care of EARL SIMMONS, because I know Sharon is one of the best nurses on the planet, period. I recall other highly skilled Doctors and nurses turning to her every day for professional advice.

ALL MY BEAUTIFUL LOVING WIFE AND I CARED ABOUT WAS HELPING OTHERS.

One day while resting at home my wife was searching YouTube. I will never forget this day. I was laying across the bed and Sharon was sitting in her favorite chair. She was just searching, and don't you know suddenly, this song came up on her phOne. She showed me her phone and said look what came up on my phone. She said, "do you know this group." She knew I love gospel music and I would know the group. I looked at her and felt GOD'S presence in the room. I said, "no I don't know this gospel group." So, Sharon played the song, and it was the most beautiful song we ever heard. THE GROUP IS CALLED "RONICA AND THE MIGHTY BLAZING STARS" out of NORTH CAROLINA.

The song that my wife fell in love with is called "LORD IT'S IN YOUR HANDS." I am so proud of this song, and it fits our life so well. When I took Sharon to work, she had to hear her song.

When I picked her up from work, I was playing her song. I told Sharon what the odds are of living almost three thousand miles from the east coast, where the group came from and have find this song. Well, this happened 30 days before Sharon would have surgery. She song her song up until her surgery as our GOD was preparing her to leave this old world. I remember and never will forget my loving mother and nephew played Sharon's song throughout the house the night before my wife homegoing service and I will never forget that. If anybody get a chance to listen to this song, I'm certain it will bless your soul.

Trust me when your GOD'S CHILD, HE will take care of HIS own.

I can recall all the close calls with DEATH as all truck drivers can, but the adventures of being on the road to service the public is priceless. I remember having to deliver truck parts to a supplier down in North Carolina. It had rain for about 3 days nonstop, so as you can imagine it was very muddy. I made my delivery and got stuck when I was in the process of picking up my empty trailer. The security officer came over and checked on me when he seen I couldn't get out.

The officer told me that I would have to call for a wrecker to pull the truck out the mud and I was in a hole that was getting deeper from the spinning of the tires. Well, the spirit of GOD calms me down and then I prayed. I began to hear from heaven, and I took a stick and used that stick to push much dirt as I could around the drive tires and I also had some chains for snow. I used the chains as if I was in the snow and I was able to gain some traction and I rock the truck back and forth. Mind you its at 11:30 at night when I'm doing this. I was able to get out the hole and out the mud and it didn't take but 5 minutes after the chains I put on. I worked the entire time doing the height of the covid pandemic delivering mail on the tractor trailer and delivering food to major retailer's and grocery stores. People would be outside the stores cheering to see me and that made me feel very proud of my job. I have had so many adventures that I couldn't collect them all in this book, but no worries I will put them in my next book that will be on my transportation career. Until this present day, I continue to work and drive to service America. One day while on my way to Pennsylvania to deliver, I would always come across this group of Amish kids on there way to school. They were on there horse and carriage ride. When I approached them on the big truck, I would be so ever careful; and careful not to startle their horse. Don't you know that they appreciate me showing them respect and would just be smiling and waving at me.

Even in the mist of whatever I'm dealing with and going through, I love and respect and reverence GOD and all people.

I can't wait to show some of the places I have been in my next book. Most places you would never know existed, because I definitely didn't know a lot of places existed till, I seen them with my own eyes and still in amazement. Till next time may the grace of GOD be with us all. And let us pray for one another.

Like I said I have seen more death than I care to see. Please be careful on the roads and be safe and courteous. Remember truck driving is not just a job but a lifestyle that good men and women live every day. I have had judges, and lawyers, doctors and even a senator and a governor, they all said thank you for the job you do and that means a lot to me. So, truck drivers keep on trucking. Do a good job and be safe!!!!!!!

Sermon
A toxic wasteland

A toxic wasteland. This planet has become a vast wasteland. Imagine if you will, a planet with no human life. Only animal and plant life and rock and land life. If this was the case, the planet would be a perfect place, minus human life. The very most important part of the Bible is genesis 6th chapter and the 5 th through the 7th verse. Verse 5 say, "and God saw that the wickedness of man was great in the earth, and that every imagination of the thoughts of his heart was only evil continually."

Verse six say; "and it repented the LORD that he had made man on the earth, and it grieved him at his heart."

Verse seven say; "and the LORD said, I will destroy man whom I have created from the face of the earth; both man and beast, and the creeping thing, and the fowl of the air; for it repenteth me that I have made them.

Somebody will ask, well pastor what makes this the greatest and most important part of the whole Bible. It plainly tells us who made us and because of man's evil and wickedness that this will happen again. The world will be destroyed again but not by water but with fire and brimstone there surely will be wailing and gnashing of teeth.

Genesis chapter 6 versus 11 and 12. Verse 11 says; "the earth also was corrupt before God and the earth was filled with violence."

Verse 12 says; "and God looked upon the earth, and, behold, it was corrupt; for all flesh had corrupted his way upon the earth." The whole purpose for Jesus coming into this world was and is to give us a way out of destruction that is quickly approaching. I for one love and thank God for giving me a way out of destruction and to have eternal life with him. This is not a cliché; God is so wonderful loving and kind. We did not create ourselves or each other.

We did not derive from any other form of life, but God. Time is winding up and coming to an end very fast like never before. thank on this, whatever time you have left on this planet whether it be 10/15/20 a hundred years, even that time it's short and God will rapture you out of this flesh body and the flesh will go back to the dust of the earth. That 's why Christ warns us to be you ready for we know not the day nor the hour.

This planet has become so polluted and toxic. The water is not safe to drink anymore. Our food is poisoned with toxins. The air we breathe is toxic, this planet has truly become a toxic wasteland at the hands of man and women. Playing with God days are over and to be honest they never should have started. Everybody claims to know and love God just like they did back in the days of Noah during the flood. But I want everyone to know that God has people, a specific people, they are called the Elect. This group of people are God's people.

I'm not going to take up too much time in my message, but GOD is soon to destroy this planet and I want my savior to be pleased with me. GOD is the potter, and we are the clay. Isaiah the 64th chapter and the 8th verse say "But now, O Lord, thou art our father; we are the clay, and thou, our potter; and we all are the work of thy hand.

Jeremiah the 18th chapter and the 2nd to the 6th verse say "Arise, and go down to the potters house, and there I will cause thee to hear my words". Verse 3 says "Then I went down to the potters house, and behold, he wrought a work on the wheels". Verse 4 says "And the vessel that he made of clay was marred in the hand of the potter; so, he made it again another vessel, as seemed good to the potter to make it". Verse 5 says "then the word of the lord came to me, saying". Verse 6 says "O house of Israel, cannot I do with you as the potter? Saith the Lord, Behold, as the clay is in the potter's hands, so are ye in mine hand, O house of Israel.

Praise GOD for making us over into a born-again human. In my case GOD took a blob of nothing clay and placed me up on his potter wheel. The good master then started to spend HIS wheel, and as I spent, and rotated, pieces of old bad clay stared to fly off me. Things like hate, arrogance, disobedient, heartless, slanderous, mean, unkind and the list goes on. Well, the potter then saw that I was ready to receive some new clay to be added to me as I spent up on HIS wheel. The potter threw new clay onto me, like LOVE, respect, caring, patience, and I can go on but, somebody gets what I'm saying. And the Potter took HIS sculping tool and mad me all over and I praise and glorify my LORD.

IN the King James version of the HOLY bible, James the 19th through the 27th verse tells us "Wherefore, my beloved brethren, let every man be swift to hear, slow to speak, slow to wrath: verse 20 say "for the wrath of man worketh not the righteousness of GOD". Verse 21 say "Wherefore lay apart all filthiness and superfluity of naughtiness, and receive with meekness the engrafted word, which is able to save your souls".

Verse 22 say; "But be ye doers of the word, and not hearers only, deceiving your own selves". Verse 23 say; "For if any be a hearer of the word, and not a doer, he is like unto a man beholding his natural face in a glass". Verse 24 say; For he beholdeth himself, and goeth his way, and straightway forgetteth what manner of man he was". Verse 25 say; "But whoso looketh into the perfect law of Liberty, and continueth therein, he being not a forgetful hearer, but a doer of the work, this man shall be blessed in his deed".

Verse 26 say; "if any man among you seem to be religious, and Bridleth not his tongue, but deceiveth his own heart, this man's religion is vain". And verse 27 says; "pure religion and undefiled before GOD and the Father is this, to visit the Fatherless and widows in their affliction, and to keep himself unspotted from the world". GOD is real, and so is every word that the LORD said.

What a waste. This is what GOD who created everything is saying to HIMSELF. The bible lets us know that from the beginning of time, men and women fell the creator and broke HIS heart. The thing about life and creation is that we as humans are the heart of GOD. Every beautiful thing that makes your physical appearance up, came from GOD the CREATORS HEART. While we hate and murder one another for absolutely no reason at all, GODs love for us stay consistent.

In spite of all my sins and imperfection, GOD has always taken care of me, HIS child. When I was right and even when I was completely and totally wrong, the savior took care of me.

Through seen and unseen dangers. When I was places that I had no business being at, GOD always took care of me, and let no hurt, nor harm or danger destroy me, and I thank my LORD.

People that profess they know GOD need to show it and most of all separate themselves from this toxic and trifling and doomed world. JESUS declared during HIS time here on earth that the words of GOD have went completely all over the earth and that GOD will not revise, revamp, modify, HIS words for no one. This is a very sick and confusing world in so much that GODs word says, "As in the days of Noah, so shall it be" and these days and times are much worst today. We the elect are living in a world where you have wolves walking around in sheep clothing, seeking whom they may devour and kill. Meanwhile the elite and the powers to be the powers and principalities have the chokehold on the children of God.

Time is coming to an end very fast, like never before. People's hearts are failing them young and old. People are in a state of confusion like I have never seen. Everybody has seemed to have lost there way as we travel through this sorrow valley of DEATH.

Proverbs the 29th chapter and the 2nd verse tells us plainly, "when the righteous are in authority, the people rejoice; but when the wicked beareth rule, the people mourn". Take a moment to think about this most powerful scripture and I'm sure that just like me you have seen this a lot in our land and worldwide. What Elite, or high power, or principalities, and so on, do you think that they actually know what love is? They know what the love of their little fortune is and that's the extent of their life. They don't have a clue as to what love is. They can make movies and write all the books and do all the talk shows they want, but it's all TALK. LOVE is an ACTION that all the money and silver and gold in this world CAN NOT buy.

LOVE is a seed that must be planted in your body and soul by the creator and sustainer of life.

I worship and praise my GOD for planting the seed of love in me and it took roots and bloomed into something beautiful.

This earth is so toxic with hate and evil and evildoers, are at an all time high to bring hurt, harm and danger to men, women, and children all over the world. What amazes me the most as a child of GOD is this; Every December 25th people all over the world celebrate the birth of JESUS CHRIST, and claim to know and love HIM, but 364 days they live for this world. Just one day a year, out of the 365 days. Every where you look today there is somebody thinking they can prophecy. Well, here is the only true prophecy, if you don't be born again and take on a baby's heart that knows no ill, then you will hear the voice of the only true GOD above that says, "I CREATED". Yes, you will finally hear from GOD, and you will be in his presence, you will look GOD face to face and eye to eye, and for so many who just knew they was on the right track, GOD will say "depart from me, ye that work iniquity.

What the false prophets, and false teachers and evildoers won't tell you is the truth and that is because they are of their farther the DEVIL. The truth is we are at war. That's why GODs word tell us so many times to put on the whole armor of GOD. We are warned by Jesus, to be wise as the serpent.

This day and time you can't find nobody doing battle for our LORD, and you surely don't see GOD in nobody that "proclaim" they know GOD. This is what me and my beloved beautiful daughter of GOD, we teached and preached, sung and prayed every day of our life on this Battlefield.

What SATAN don't want nobody to know is the truth. The truth is we have been at war and there are only a few true believers.

The BIBLE say to be a friend of this world is to be an enemy of GOD. My darling sister JOYCE, lead people to GOD, and I found out many years' latter by these people that their life was changed, and they say that GOD saved them because of my sister JOYCE. My wife SHARON and my sister JOYCE are in their new bodies that don't require oxygen and don't require food to eat for energy. They continue to do battel for GOD, and they are a present help to those in need when GOD almighty sends them to help HIS children. How do I know this. The words of GOD say to be absent from the body is to be present with GOD. When the man asked JESUS to remember him when he enters into HIS FATHERS KIGDOM, and JESUS said, "this day", not tomorrow, not wait here till I come back, JESUS said "THIS DAY" shalt thou be with me in paradise.

I am working for this paradise for myself and others. I LOVE THE LORD!!!!

And GOD didn't tell me nor anyone else that this walk trough this valley and shadows of death walk would be a bed of Roses.

Instead, my savior told us that man born of a woman is of a few days and them days will be full of trouble.

The best part about life is that if we hold on and fight the good fight of faith and lay hold on eternal life, JESUS has a REWARD for us. Yes, I suffer in my body from stage 4 sarcoidosis, but being on GODs battlefield, we will be injured and killed. All the saints of GOD have been wounded on the battlefield.

And one of my favorite scriptures is ROMANS 8 chapter and the 18 verse say "For I reckon that the sufferings of this present time are not worthy to be compared with the glory which shall be revealed in us". I don't mind suffering, GOD haven't removed my stumbling blocks, but HE has led me all around them, and I praise and thank my LORD. This is my JOB to give GODs word that someone may turn from their evil ways. God's words will not return to HIM void, but shall accomplish that which HE please. And you can't see heavenly things? You never seen an angel of GOD? Well think on this, my FATHER who are in heaven, can HIS holy spirit ever enter in your body?

We know that its not the things that go into a person, but its what comes out of there heart and mouth that defile that person. Can the spirit of GOD ever enter you or are people heart and mouth and soul just so filthy with so much mess that the spirit of GOD can't enter and show them anything. Please understand and I know people think the spirit of GOD in them and all that, but the truth is there is a spirit in a lot of people, but its not the spirit of my SAVOIR. Truth is there is so much evil, all people are doing is DECIEVING themselves. I'm not going to be long, and I will get to my sermon, because all that I say and do, is because I love every single soul on this planet, period.

John 15 chapter and the 13th verse say, "Greater love hath no man than this, that a man lay down his life for his friends". can only pray and hope that somebody is getting GODs word.

With this being the greatest LOVE, don't you know that the greatest miracle is like this; To love somebody that hates you is the greatest miracle, and JESUS performed this out on the cross. This world indeed is a toxic wasteland, that is soon to be consumed by fire and there will be a great pain in the earth like never known to any man.

You need to get your heart right with GOD, because only the pure in heart shall see GOD. Remember that scripture?

But get your heart right, because the LORD is calling us to quickly come before HIM and answer all that we have done this little time on the earth; to answer for every action and every Idle word that men shall speak, whether they be good or bad.

Please draw close to GOD and HE will draw close to you.

Remember Psalms 27chapter and the 10th verse says, "When my father and my mother forsake me, then the LORD will take me up. And pray for forgiveness. Don't worry about what religion is going to heaven and what day is the sabbath on and all these things. We are all guilty of denying our first true and only love and that's GOD our CREATOR. We all have broken and abandoned the very first of all commandments, and because of this we are guilty of breaking all and every commandment that our LOVING FATHER has given. Please repent and pray. Please.

Galatians the 6th chapter and the 3 rd and 4th verse says, "For if a man think himself to be something, when he is nothing, he deceiveth himself". "But let every man prove his own work, and then shall he have rejoicing in himself alone, and not in another."

GOD can care less about your degrees, and there is nothing wrong with getting a higher education, but in all your getting, please get an understanding. The highest degree any man or woman can receive comes from the only one that has all knowledge and produce knowledge in us. That knowledge is that the creator made us and not we ourselves. And someone may say in a silly sarcastic manner "wow that's deep knowledge", but the truth is if anybody just knew that, then people would act on it and the world would be a better place to live, without all these killings all the time. IF people really knew a creator made us, then they would fear HIM in a loving righteous way and would live better. GOD is LOVE. HE showed the world HIS LOVE by bringing EVERY HUMAN into EXISTANCE and the world TURNED there back on the SAVIOR. Jeremiah the 3 rd chapter and the 14th verse tells us and this is GOD who CREATED speaking and HE say "TURN, O BACKSLIDING CHILDREN, SAITH THE LORD; FOR I AM MARRIED UNTO YOU: AQND I WILL TAKE YOU ONE OF A CITY, AND TWO OF A FAMILY, AND I WILL BRING YOU TO ZION:" GOD has given us a way out and its up to us to walk through that door.

People don't know what love is, they do not have clue. They know what conditional love is, they know what obsession is. The world, the ELITE, and the powers in high places have a sick twisted agenda that goes against GOD our FATHER. What I am proposing and trying to offer is something more than all the money in the world, and something silver and gold can't buy.

The ELECT of GOD, which are only a few, possess this real true love. I am offering this world LOVE just like JESUS did. TRY GOD AND SEE FOR YOURSELF. My wife minister SHARON KAYE FITZGERALD and I was EQUALLY YOKED with GOD our master and when HE joined us together, we were EQUALLY YOKED together and had a wonderful life and love each other like I have never seen LOVE in a relationship. A man is very important in a boy's life, I was denied that. Growing up I seen some days when I would be hungry, I survived that. I have been lied on and talked about; I survived through all that. What I'm trying to say is that because of my LORD GOD 'I I MADE IT." Through the storm and through the rain, "I MADE IT." GOD HAS NEVER LET GO OF MY HAND NEVER. i am trying to offer the same to whoever want GODs LOVE in their life. PROVERBS 14 chapter and the 12th verse say, "THERE IS A WAY WHICH SEEMETH RIGHT UNTO A MAN, BUT THE END THEREOF ARE THE WAYS OF

DEATH." THE GREAT MASS OF PEOPLE ARE TRAPPED IN THIS CYCLE AND THINK THEY KNOW GOD AND WHAT LOVE IS, BUT THEY STILL FOOLING THEMSELVES.

GOD IS THE ONLY ONE YOU CAN DEPEND ON, PEOPLE HAVE MARKED GOD AND CRITICIZED HIS PEOPLE AND HAS PHYSICALLY AND VERBALY ABUSED GODS LOVED ONES. THIS SICK TWISTED WORLD HAS BLASPHEMED ON GOD AND HIS SPIRIT AND THINK GOD HEARS YOU WHEN YOU PRAY, AND THINK HE ANSWER YOUR PRAYER. SOMETHING MAY HEAR YOU PRAY AND GRANT YOUR WISHES, BUT GOD AND HIS WORDS ARE NOT COMPROMISED NEVER. GOD DOES NOT GO BACK ON HIS WORDS FOR NOBODY AND WHEN HEAVEN AND EARTH PASS GOD'S WORDS WILL STILL STAND. WE ARE IN A LAUGH NOW CRY LATER SITUATION, AS FOR ME AND MY HOUSE WILL ALWAYS SERVE MY GOD. I GIVE ALL HONOR TO MY LORD FOR TEACHING ME HOW TO BUILD MY HOUSE UPON HIS ROCK AND THE GATES OF HELL SHALL NOT PPREVAIL AGAINST ME.

GOD IS SICK TO HIS STOMACH WITH THIS TOXIC, TRIFLING WORLD. YOU CAN'T SERVE GOD AND THIS WORLD TOO, GOD SAY BECAUSE YOU ARE LUKEWARM, HE WILL SPEW YOU OUT OF HIS MOUTH. TO THOSE CHILDREN OF GOD WHO HOLD OUT TILL THE END, GREAT IS OUR REWARD. I FOR ONE ALWAYS LIKE TO GET A REWARD FOR MY WORK. I LOVE EVERY SiNGLE HUMAN GOD HAS CREATED. WE ARE ALL SPECIAL TO THE LORD AND CAN NEVER BE NOTHING BUT A CHILD TO GOD, THINK ABOUT IT.

Why waste your time in this old deceitful, perverted, trifling and toxic waste world. No matter where you get your daily information on current events from, its all a LIE! The demonic powers and forces must keep the public in fear and entertained. Their rumors of wars and talk shows and drama shows and false and fake entertainment. We the elect of GOD, have something money can't buy and the great mass need. We have real unconditional love for everybody and a peace that passes all understanding.

All that I have been through in my life, I am glad to say, "I have made it." Life is short, and eternity is forever so you decide. GOD has always stood by myside when I was right and when I was wrong. I'm glad I turned my back on everything and made GOD my only focus. I'm almost done with my sermon, but the truth is you only pass this way one time and when you leave there is no coming back. Hell is very real as well, believe or don't believe. I personally don't want to find out firsthand, because there are people by the unheard-of numbers down there.

One last thing and I will be done, GOD is real. Let me take my time and explain HIS existence for those who just don't understand. We all did not come into this physical world but instead born into a spiritual world. That's why the spirits have power over the flesh. Sadly, most of the spirits are demonic in this world, evil spirits. People are DEMONIC POSSESSED just like GODs word tells us. Just live through a day on earth and you sure to find that this is all the way truth. Now how we know GOD is real, when you are hungry you can't see that you are you just feel that you are. When pain is in your body, you can't see the pain, but you know that it's there. You can't see the wind softly blowing against your skin, but you can feel it. You can't see the cold, but you can feel its cold. You can't see the most important thing on this earth for human existence, and that's "1-120." This is our oxygen and without it all life will end up existing. GOD is a spirit and exist in the spirit, You can feel HIM and see HIM in everything HE created. All the animals, and plants and rock life and every human being are beautiful. How I know my savior lives, because this GOD that I humbly bow myself down before, HE is the most hated and despised of all the GODs. Nobody, or shall I say just a few, cares to seek his face. And all this "MEGA" this, and "MEGA" that continue in your miss leading those who would be ELECT CHILDREN OF GOD. GREAT IS YOUR REWARD IN DAMNATION, See the world LOVE your sounding brass speeches, with no life in what you're teaching. GODs word in Matthew the 10th chapter and 22nd verse says, "AND YE SHALL BE HATED OF ALL MEN FOR MY NAME'S SAKE: BUT HE THAT ENDURETH TO THE END SHALL BE SAVED." And you can feel when you're saved because the old things in you are gone, AMAN!!! People despise my GOD; they take HIS name in vain like drinking HIS water that our body must have. They lie on my GOD, and they form HIS words to fit their little wicked agenda. One of these false prophets that preach and teach to BILLIONS of people and evangelize all over the world and blow his bad breath in people face and the fall out, and he tap them on the forehead, and they fall out, this one came forward and confessed that he never healed anybody by GOD's power. He said it's all entertainment, but that's blaspheming in the highest form. The sad part is that he is still doing it today. One false prophet and his wife were busted for wearing earpieces while working the crowd, pretending to prophesy. One false prophet told the world GOD ordered him to raise $8 million dollars or he will die. People are so naive and gullible, but they will fall for anything, and these demonic forces know this. This may be the false prophets last warning, but Ezekiel 13th chapter and the 3rd verse GOD is SPEAKING and say,

"THUS SAITH THE LORD GOD; WOE UNTO THE FOOLISH PROPHETS, THAT FOLLOW THEIR OWN SPIRIT, AND HAVE SEEN NOTHING!"

I'm not done yet because this message just might save someone's life! Another well known false prophet told the world to destroy all his books, CDs and cassette tapes on tithing, because he was wrong. Woe unto all these false prophets. JEREMIAH THE 23RD CHAPTER AND THE 1ST- 2nd VERSE SAY, "WOE BE UNTO THE PASTORS THAT DESRTOY AND SCATTER THE SHEEP OF MY PASTURE! SAITH THE LORD, THEREFORE THUS SAITH THE LORD GOD OF ISRAEL AGAINST THE PASTORS THAT FEED MY PEOPLE; YE HAVE SCATTERED MY FLOCK, AND DRIVEN THEM AWAY, AND HAVE NOT VISITED THEM: BEHOLD, I WILL VISIT UPON YOU THE EVIL OF YOUR DOINGS, SAITH THE LORD." GOD has warned these mega false prophets and apostles and bishops and evangelist and so on, because they like big names, GOD is longsuffering, but will only take but so much of false mess. I think how one pastor preach and told the whole church that he is homosexual, and didn't make it home right after church, but ran head on with a TRACTOR TRAILER and died. One false prophet I seen preaching and sweating like he knew GOD personally. Well, he manages to empty the church bank account and leave the state with the secretary, and they went to California where he would quickly get sick and die. One lady come home from church and pastor had blown his head off with a 12 gauge in the back yard. One that I knew that seemed to everybody, to have known GOD the FATHER, this one was found completely nude and floating in the lake.

One in Alabama gave most of his church members AIDS. Another false pastor I visit the church with family cheated on his wife. When she came home and caught him in their bed with another woman, well the wife pulled out her pistol and shot pastor in the feet. When it went to court the judge told the wife "You should have killed him," and in the eyes of the law and with GOD, being "UNFAITHFUL" is a very serious crime.

I know a lot more situations that has happen to pastors leading GODs sheep wrong, I mean what more can I say, GOD is a man of his word, and he gave HIS warning. I can't make this stuff up if I tried on my best day, this is just the world we live in now. We must turn back to GOD, our first true love. This is how I know beyond a shadow of doubt that GOD is very real. Men and women who profess to know him spend to much time playing with HIM, like a child with a loaded gun. Somebody is going to get hurt. One mega pastor star has a water gun and shoots water or oil, which ever they are feeling that day, and shooting it at the congregation. One preacher say that she has tattoos and going to get more, when GODs word plainly tells us not to mark up our bodies. And like you have them put on; they can be removed the same way. JEREMIAH 5TH CHAPTER AND THE 31ST VERSE, PLAIN AS LIGHT, TELLS US, "THE PROPHETS PROPHESY

FALSELY, AND THE PRIESTS BEAR RULE BY THEIR MEANS; AND MY PEOPLE LOVE TO HAVE IT SO: AND WHAT WILL YE DO IN THE END THEREOF?"

GOD said "MY PEOPLE LOVE TO HAVE IT SO" this is why nobody can honestly communicate with our LORD or see angels and have GOD reveal anything to nobody, because people are letting to much play mess go ona There is no order in the house of GOD. And being that our bodies are the true house of GOD, there is no order in our HEART, MIND, AND SOUL!

I can only pray that this message that GOD has given me, reach somebody's heart and soul. I hope that GOD TURN somebody around and start them to walking towards HIM. I FELT THE POWER OF MY GOD IN THIS MESSAGE AND GODS WORD CUT LIKE A TWO EDGE SWORD, AND FATHER GOD, I THANK YOU FOR CORRECTION. What I'm trying to say is when you preach one thing and live another, you're in danger.

DON'T YOU KNOW, that in the spirit you can do more than in the flesh. I'm almost done with my sermon, but people don't know what happens to you when you pass out of this life, and the HOLY BIBLE tells us exactly what happens. When your heart stops pumping blood from one vein to the other, and your brain goes dead, your soul that lived in that flesh for however long, it separates itself and goes back to the one that joined your soul into the flesh at the time of birth. All of this takes place in the blink of an eye. It's in GODs word, but what happens next is the most tragic part for a lot of people. Before you can blink your eye, you are beholding your creator. We all know that you can't kill a soul or your spirit so it will live forever somewhere. Now you are standing in front of a jealous GOD, with a broken heart, because most people refuse or just don't know how to worship and serve GOD in the spirit, but now its time to answer for all you done. At this point one of two things are about to happen. One is that you had honestly repented, and GOD excepted you to live, and for HIM in peace forever. Well, the next thing is not such a good outcome! The second thing is that GOD rejected you because you never needed the creator, and you were your own GOD or had another GOD. At this point you will be cast into outer darkness and your soul will burn in a fire that never can go out. There will be wailing and gnashing of teeth, DON'T YOU KNOW all of this takes place in the blink of an eye. Before they can toe tag you at the morgue, you have moved on to your final place and that's life. In the medical profession, when my loving wife SHARON was working as a NURSE in the nursing homes, I had the opportunity to witness when she had to call the time of death on people who had passed away. She hated that part of her job most of all, but it was her job. Someone will call our time of death, so it pays to treat people right, you know, the way we expect to be treated. Like I said, you can do more in the spirit than in the flesh. Sharon knew this, and I preach and teach it everywhere I go. You may not believe this, but children of GOD know what I'm talking about, you can feel the presence of GOD's ANGELS around us. My wife and I had an opportunity to have an ANGEL come to us, and it's the most HOLY thing to ever happen to us. Well, I had been praying for a long time on how to write my first book and who shall publish it, because this book is not just about my life, but also contain this message from GOD. While resting at my leisure, I could faintly hear my sweet wife saying "you got to get your book out, the world needs to know. I began to reason within myself how, and I didn't know what to do. "DON'T YOU KNOW, I am always online looking for things to order and on this particular day suddenly, right out of the blue, my wife's book pops up on the screen. I clicked on the book, and it took me to amazon. The book was being sold on amazon and published by AUTHOR HOUSE PUBLISHING. The joy I had made me speechless. DON'T YOU KNOW I ordered that book; it was the only copy. Not only the last copy, but it was signed in my wife's handwriting, and I never owned a copy of her first book, which was published 8 months before she met me, So, things came together very quickly for me to get my story to the world, and this is what she wanted.

I'm about to wrap my message up but be careful what you feed your body and soul, please. If you read a book and it should help you, but there is no change in your life, then that book is worthless. Please be aware of the wolves going around through this earth in sheep clothing. The wolf has blended in with the sheep to kill and devour the sheep. My lovely wife and I, like to go shopping at the garage sales and street market. While visiting the street market in Augusta, Georgia, we seen a guy in a motorized wheelchair. He had written a book and was selling it for $40 dollars and Sharon bought a book from him to support this guy. I just had a not so good feeling about this. So, we leave and I'm driving down the road and Sharon is reading this book. The very next thing I knew, Sharon seen a dumpster and told me to pull up to the dumpster and she threw that book away. I said why you toss the book into the dumpster. She said that book was pure trash, hot garbage. Sharon said that the guy talks about when he was a big-time drug dealer, and all the money he made and fancy cars he had, but what really got to my wife was when he talked about, in detail how he abused women. She said he could make women do some very gross things and this is what his book about. He was bragging and bosting on his drug king days. This guy in the wheelchair was paralyzed from the neck down, and he was this way from a shoot-out.

Your sins will find you out. That's what the elders would say about this situation. One Christ the solid rock I stand, All other ground is sinking sand. So please remember that we are to love and care for one another with pure unconditional, and unwavering "LOVE." I can hear somebody saying when was the last time LOVE paid anybody's bills. As a child of GOD, I can say a lot of times GOD made a way for me. (IF YOU KNOW, YOU KNOW). In my condition doing the very best that I can, my wife and I have helped more people of all races and ETHNICITIES, because of GOD's LOVE. Everybody loves to quote JOHN 3:16, "for GOD so love the world," and HE did, but what did the world do? The world turned there back on their first love, and this broke GOD's heart, forever. They turned to strange gods, and some consider themselves to be a god.

I love GOD and he is a MAN of his words.

Remember Matthew the 25th chapter and the 45th verse.

"Then shall he answer them, saying, verily I say unto you, inasmuch as ye did it not to one of the least of these, ye did it not to me."

JESUS is letting you know that we are responsible for each other's wellbeing. It dose not matter who you are, no matter who's you are, when the LORD come and call you up out of this earth and this life, there is one thing that you will not be able to do, and that is REFUSE, the LORD GOD. What's funny to me is that the RICH, WEALTH, ELITES think that they are IMMUNE from GOD's wrath, and can treat people any kind of way that they want. When in all reality, this group of people are the major cause for GOD's wrath. For they are the principalities in high places all over the world, raining down havoc on God's children. I MUST SAY THAT I LOVE EACH AND EVERY LIVING SOUL ON THIS PLANET. THERE WILL COME A NEW HEAVEN AND A NEW EARTH SOME DAY. TILL THEN WE MUST FALL IN LINE AND DISCOVER WHAT LOVE IS. THIS IS THE MOST DIFFICULT THING IN THE WORLD TO DO, BECAUSE YOU CAN'T MISS WHAT YOU NEVER HAD. MOST PEOPLE NEVER HAD LOVE AND CAN'T GIVE WHAT THEY NEVER HAD. THE WORLD CAN'T GIVE IT IF THAT'S WHERE YOU'RE LOOKING. ONLY GOD CAN GIVE IT AND TO GET IT YOU MUST BE SINCER WITH A CHILDLIKE HEART.

REMEMER THERE IS NOTHING NEW UNDER THE SUN, THE SAME LIES AND DE-CIE-T AND UNRULY THAT'S GOING ON IN THE CHURCH NOW HAS BEEN GOING ON, ITS JUST NEW PLAYERS. I AM SEEING GOD PURGING THIS WICKED WORLD OF THESE OLD FALSE PREACHERS AND TEACHERS. THEY ARE GOING TO ANSWER FOR THE SCATTERING OF GOD'S PEOPLE. SOON, AND VERY SOON THEY ARE GOING TO ANSWER TO THE MOST HIGH.

JUST A FEW MORE THINGS THEN I'LL BE DONE WITH GOD'S MESSAGE

I remember one day when I was on my way to the largest retailer in the world. It was a hot Saturday evening, and I was pulling up to this store. When I pulled up to this store there was an oriental man and an oriental woman, and they had a 3-yearold boy. The man was holding up a posterboard sign saying that they have a baby in the hospital that needed surgery on the brain. DON'T YOU KNOW, I went into this store and could not remember what I was in there for, thinking about the couple outside. Well, I went to my car and had started to leave, but in my mind, I could see my wife smiling, because she knew what I was going to do. I pulled up at the light and the guy looked at me and I opened my window and gave him $600 dollars cash. This kind man just broke down in tears. He showed his wife, and she burst into tears. I don't care who you are, I have always helped people, because it's in my heart. What little I have I will share, but the best thing I can offer anybody is the love of GOD. The one and only one who can set us free from sin. I love my indigenous brothers and sisters, the only true natives to this land. My wife Sharon and I have always loved to serve the natives of this land and eat with them. I remember on Sunday at their church they had me preach for the first time at there church and this just blew my mind because the natives do not let outsiders into their world, and that's because their world is sacred and clean and pure. On this day that I preached the chief, or the leader of the tribe was in attendance, and he have taken pitchers at the white house with presidents. This was a huge honor for me as anyone can imagine.

My wife and I and our children were a big help to the Indians. See on the reservation they have their own belief in a powerful GOD. A medicine man or medicine woman is a traditional healer and spiritual LEADER who serves a community of indigenous people of the Americas. During times of illness many NATIVE AMERICANS will call upon a medicine man or woman or shaman, in most cases the medicine person is also considered a HOLY person because it is the belief that they do all their healing with the creator's help and guidance. I have prayed and asked our lord GOD to heal many of our brother's and sister's and GOD healed. So, when the medicine man found that I was asking our LORD, GOD to heal the natives, the medicine man wanted to meet with me. GOD was touching and healing and brining back those who would be dead if not for our praying, and that's what the native American's were saying about me. Hundreds of people GOD touched. The medicine man said, your able to pray to GOD and HE touch and heal my people. A lot of medicine man on different reservations said the same thing. They got to see and experience the real power of GOD, and it made me proud. I truly know GOD in a HOLY and DEVINE way. The natives on a few reservations asked if I would be their pastor and lead them. I haven't heard this testimony from anybody, and that's because the Natives don't associate with this sick, file and toxic land we live in. The natives are a loving, greatly respected, loving GOD and HIS planet people. The natives of all the tribes are beautiful people.

I'm almost done with this message that GOD gave me, but what I have to offer is the same thing JESUS tried to offer this old world and that is how to LOVE. Again, LOVE is something money can't buy and more precious than silver and gold.

Divine LOVE is imperative to this life just like oxygen we need to breathe in our body.

Divine LOVE is imperative as H20, or water we need for our drink.

Love is just as important as food we need to survive.

Your life needs love to survive.

I'm going to wrap up this message with just one thought.

There is a sickness that has taken over this planet and you need to protect you and your children and family from this deadly disease. This disease takes over the heart and brain and is killing people like never before seen or heard of. As long as I can remember I would like to gaze up at the moon at night. I often say that if the moon could talk it would have a long list of things that it has seen happen on this earth.

The deadly disease that I am referring to is HATE. This disease HATE has killed more people than anything. I'm sure everybody is aware of this sickness, so I won't go into detail about it, but know that GOD is the only cure for this disease. Please know and understand that GOD WILL NOT go back on his word not for anybody, and HIS word can't be COMPROMISED no matter what comes and goes.

I was just thinking on how to end this message FAIL US LORD. YOU CAN'T LIE, DEAR GOD YOUR WORD IS YOUR BOND BETWEEN US AND YOU, DEAR GOD AND IT WILL NOT, YOUR WORDS WILL NOT, RETURN TO YOU VOID GOD. PLEASE MY LORD, GOD CLEAN MY HEART AND MY MIND FROM ALL SICK, EVIL, HATE, AND MAKE ME CLEAN INSIDE GOD AND FILL ME WITH YOUR HOLY SPIRIT AND MAKE ME HOLY FOR YOU ARE HOLY GOD. LORD GOD BE MY GUIDE FOR EVER AND EVER AMEN.

MAY THE GRACE OF OUR GOD, REST, RULE, AND ABIDE IN YOU FOREVER AND FOREVER.

I LOVE YOU ALL AND THANK YOU ALL.

AND WHEN TIMES GET ROUGH AND LOTS OF TIMES YOU CAN'T SEE NO WAY OUT, HOLD ON PLEASE. JUST HOLD ON.

WHEN PAIN ALL IN YOUR BODY AND DOCTORS CAN'T HELP YOU, IF YOU CAN, JUST LOOK UP TO THE SKY AND SMILE. TELL THE CREATOR THAT YOU ARE WILLING TO WAIT ON HIM.

THANK YOU, GOD, FOR EVERYTHING. AND GOD, BE OUR JOY FOR EVER AND EVER.

I LOVE YOU ONE AND ALL, SEE YOU IN CHURCH!

PLEASE REMEMBER ONE THING. FAMILY AND FRIENDS WILL ALWAYS BREAK YOUR HEART. DON'T YOU KNOW I HAVE HAD SOME PAIN IN MY BODY AND 1M SURE MANY PEOPLE HAVE.

THERE IS NO PAIN LIKE HAVING YOUR HEART BROKEN BY PEOPLE WHO CLAIM TO LOVE YOU AND HAVE YOUR BEST INTREST. THIS IS A VERY TROUBLING AND TOXIC WORLD THAT WE LIVE IN CHILDREN OF GOD, BUT HOLD ON, YOU CAN MAKE IT. PEOPLE ALL AROUND US HAVING A FORM OF GODLYNESS.

SOMETIME CHILDREN OF GOD WE HAVE TO CRY ALL NIGHT LONG, MANY OF TIMES WE HAVE BEEN MADE TO CRY, BUT YOU JUST HOLD ON. GOD LOVES YOU; JESUS LOVES YOU; I LOVE YOU. OUR CRYING DAYS WILL SOON BE OVER.

WE WILL HOLD ON AND STEADFAST TOGETHER.

THERE IS NO OTHER BOOK WITH THE DEEPEST SINCERE LOVE AND HOPE, OTHER THAN THE BIBLE, THAT WILL TEACH AND HOPE THAT US AS CHILDREN OF GOD WILL WALK AND NOT FAINT. WE MUST HOLD ON AND LOVE ONE ANOTHER. WITH TIME COMING TO AN END SOON, WE ALL NEED EACH OTHER.

SO, LET'S HOLD ON AND KEEP OUR FAITH. I KNOW IT GETS HARD BUT HOLD ON WITH ME AND WE SHALL COME OUT AS MORE THAN CONQUERS. MANY DAYS AND NIGHTS SOME TIME ALL NIGHT LONG, I HAVE HAD TO CRY, BUT I HELD ON TO GODS HAND. 1M SO GLAD I DID. THANK YOU, GOD,

AND IF YOU DON'T DO NOTHING ELSE FOR ME FATHER GOD, YOU BEEN GOOD TO ME. AMEN, AMEN, AMEN. YOU CAN MAKE IT!

So, in closing I remember having jobs and working with different people. I remember hearing a saying, "you can't fix stupid." Now when I first heard this, I thought to myself what an awful thing to say. See I have heard this a lot from a lot of people and its starting to make since to me. I don't believe in calling anybody stupid, because we are all intelligent beings. I don't believe in calling anybody a fool, but Psalm 14th chapter and 1st verse tell us that a fool has said in his heart, there is no GOD. And we know there is a wonderful GOD. I know and understand that you can't help everybody.

So let the wheat and tares grow together and Jesus will do the separation. Let's pray for one another and be there for one another in a true and HOLY way and look for nothing in return.

The joy of GOD the CREATOR is more satisfying and fulfilling than anything this universe will ever come to know. You ever had a loneliness or emptiness in your heart? We all have and it's missing the joy of the LORD GOD, that's what that emptiness is. Money can't fill it, drugs can't fill it, family and friends can't fill it, your job and degrees can't fill that void in your life, only the love and joy of GOD and HE never fail!!!!!!

Thank you all!!!!!

WE at the "ROSE OF SHARON HOUSE OF PRAYER" we LOVE you all. And may GOD'S grace and love be in you forever, AMEN!!!

D E D I C A T I O N

<u>This book is dedicated to the following loved ones.</u>

GOD MY FATHER

MINISTER SHARON KAYE JONES FITZGERALD

JOYCE L. FITZGERALD ABEL

TONYA FRANCES

NATE

THE ENTIRE FAMILY OF GOD

ALL OF MY FAMILY AND FRIENDS WHO ARE GONE FROM THIS DEATH AND ARE LIVING IN LIFE, THIS BOOK IS FOR YOU,

BECAUSE I THINK OF YOU ALL EVERYDAY, TILL WE MEET AGAIN.

Printed in the United States
by Baker & Taylor Publisher Services